Googling GOD

The Religious
Landscape
of People
in their
20s and 30s

MIKE HAYES

A Busted Halo Book

Paulist Press
New York/Mahwah, NJ

Busted Halo is a ministry outreach to the many spiritual seekers in their twenties and thirties trying to find deeper meaning in their lives but whose journey often has little to do with traditional religious institutions. Busted Halo Books, written for these young adults and those who minister to them, are part of a network of media and ministry sponsored by the Paulist Fathers that includes an online magazine, BustedHalo.com, "The Busted Halo Show" on Sirius Satellite Radio, and the Busted Halo retreat ministry.

The author and publisher are grateful to those interviewed in chapters 3 and 4 who gave their permission for the material provided to be used in this publication.

Cover design by Sharyn Banks
Book design by Lynn Else

Library of Congress Cataloging-in-Publication Data

Hayes, Mike, 1970–
    Googling God : the religious landscape of people in their 20s and 30s / Mike Hayes.
        p. cm.
    Includes bibliographical references.
    ISBN-13: 978-0-8091-4487-7 (alk. paper)
    1. Spirituality—Catholic Church. 2. Christian life—Catholic authors. 3. Generation X—Religious life. 4. Generation Y—Religious life. I. Title.
    BX2350.65.H39 2007
    259'.25—dc22

                                                                2007019726

Busted Halo Books
For spiritual seekers in their twenties and thirties and those who minister to them

Published by Paulist Press
997 Macarthur Boulevard
Mahwah, New Jersey 07430

www.paulistpress.com

Printed and bound in the United States of America

CONTENTS

ACKNOWLEDGMENTS

As a first-time author, I can say this book took many minds and hands for it to reach its final destination.

Thanks go to the Paulist Fathers and the members of the staff at Paulist Press for helping me craft this book. A special word of thanks goes to my colleagues at Paulist Young Adult Ministries: Father Brett Hoover, CSP, Father Dave Dwyer, CSP, and editor-in-chief, Bill McGarvey. Each of your unique gifts has contributed to these pages in many ways. Father Michael Hunt, CSP, and my editor, Father Mike Kerrigan, CSP, helped refine the original manuscript into these pages and provided much encouragement along the way.

Second, to the staff at the Graduate School of Religion and Religious Education at Fordham University in the Bronx I offer my heartfelt gratitude. Special thanks goes to the dean, Father Anthony Sciorra, and its distinguished group of professors, especially my mentors, Dr. Kieran Scott and Father James Bacik.

My ministry colleagues from around the United States have been a wonderful resource for much of this book. Father John Cusick and Kate DeVries helped with setting the bar high for all young adult ministry models. My colleagues on the board of directors of the National Catholic Young Adult Ministry Association (NCYAMA), especially its acting director, Paul Jarzembowski, and former executive director, Michelle Miller, who provided much-needed criticism and help in securing interviews.

There are twelve interviewees in chapters 3 and 4 who courageously allowed me to tell their stories of faith. I am eternally grateful to you for letting me share your words with those who read this book. Father Jim McDermott, SJ, and Alan Grossman kept my mind sharp and free of worry during my writing and also provided generous feedback.

Finally, to my parents, Evelyn and Michael Hayes, Sr., and my sister, Kathleen: you were my first teachers of faith. I couldn't have had better models of faith in my formative years. Your words are hidden in these pages.

Last, to my loving wife, Marion, this book has robbed you of countless hours that we could have been spending together. While my ministry to young adults is very important to me, it is nothing unless I get to come home to you. I love you and dedicate this book, my first, to you.

August 28, 2006
Paulist Young Adult Ministries
New York City

FOREWORD

Significant numbers of young adult Catholics today remain loosely connected to the institutional church. The situation is similar to a malaise that has beset mainline Protestantism over the last half century—where decline and institutional tepidness are more about the failure to energize and retain the young than about the death of the old. Larger cultural dynamics are also at work. Consider the widespread assumption in our "seeker" milieu that one can be close to the divine without being close to a church.

Thanks to a confluence of factors including the visionary efforts of individuals such as Father John C. Cusick and Katherine F. DeVries in Chicago (Theology on Tap), and to initiatives such as the Paulist Young Adult Ministry (BustedHalo.com) and the National Catholic Young Adult Ministry, the importance of Catholicism's roughly twenty to forty years of age cohort is becoming more of a front-burner challenge. I use the word *challenge* to counter any erroneous idea that young adults are a "problem" in the church. *Problem* is the wrong start-up language, a label ripe with unwarranted assumptions.

Aside from their obvious importance vis-à-vis their sheer numbers (large), young adult Catholics arc significant today because their current relationship to the tradition—expressed in (sometimes) enigmatic, eclectic, and contradictory ways—predicts much about the church to come. As life-cycle research shows, it is the youth of today, not the old of today, who predict the old of tomorrow.

Those who labor in the field are aware—and common sense dictates—that young adult ministry is conditioned by various considerations. One is the obvious need to know something about the population at hand. Who are young adults? How has the prodigiously diverse American culture shaped their lives and values? What are their needs and dreams?

The starting point here is recognition that young adult Catholics are not a homogeneous group, a point often lost when they end up aggregated under "Gen X" and "Millennial" labels. As Mike Hayes wisely observes, young adults vary in multiple ways. Young adult ministry, therefore, cannot be a one-size-fits-all ministry.

A related dynamic is the need to develop effective strategies for engaging young adults. How do we "make disciples" of these new generations? What practices constitute successful outreach? What strategies yield authentic faith development, responsible appropriation of the tradition, and commitment to the ritual, sacramental, and communal dimensions so foundational to Catholic identity?

Mike Hayes's book is a boon on all of the above accounts. His interview profiles convey a rich and varied landscape of images, thoughts, and feeling animating the religious and spiritual perceptions of young adult Catholics. His own seasoned experience in young adult ministry projects a tested sense of what does and does not work. In addition, Hayes's annotated catalog of Web and Internet sources is invaluable for anyone working with a generation for whom "Googling God" is a natural part of the spiritual quest.

Young adult Catholics need to be engaged—in both their faith and in their questioning. They need opportunities to share their gifts and talents and, indeed, their ministry. Vital community experiences, sound teachings, edifying and transforming liturgies, disciplined and authentic spiritualities, and venues for social justice are core elements of this engagement. And while these elements are hardly new to the history of Catholicism, how they are configured, communicated, and received within post-modern culture and the technological revolution and within the new dimensions of the church-world relationship today surely are. Mike Hayes knows all of this well. His narrative proceeds accordingly.

Behold the challenge.

William D. Dinges
The Catholic University of America
Washington, DC
June 2006

INTRODUCTION:
PURPOSE AND METHOD

This book is for those who are dumbfounded in their attempts to understand the two most recent generations to come into adulthood, Generation X (born between 1964 and 1979) and the Millennials (born after 1980). Most especially it is for those who minister to these age groups within the Catholic Church. In an age when there is much doubt about whether young people are religious at all, there is also a religious awakening going on among young people that has taken many by surprise. The world also has become a place where technology and fast-paced media have shaped our expectations not merely about the news, but also about the way we live our everyday life. Most important, we should note that this technological age is the norm for people within their twenties and thirties (not to mention the younger generation).

Both in the Catholic Church and within the ecumenical dialogue, young adults in the United States are living in a time filled with much uncertainty and angst, as well as a thirst for instant gratification in the face of an unknown tomorrow. These two aspects of American culture need to be kept at the forefront of our minds. One needs to remember that young adults live in a noisy world filled with fast-paced communication technologies in which many, while uncertain of their future, also thrive professionally and economically. Some of the brightest minds in many realms of modern American culture are those of young adults. They are making decisions that affect companies, organizations, political policy, and the media, as well as the Catholic Church. It is important for us from the onset not to fall into the trap of defining young adults as the church's next generation. Rather, young adults are the present generation of Catholics. It is the present generation in which my approach is based. I start our journey in defining these two generations by getting inside the culture in which we all live as Americans in order to understand its influence on both Generation X and Millennials. I have found that three things will take precedence:

1. Young adults often assume that they can "Google God."

We need always to assume that a large percentage of young adults believe that instant gratification is merely a click of a mouse or a touch of a button away and that they can apply this to every area of their life, religion included. It is true that Google provides a service with which you can find virtually anything, on the Internet.

2. Understanding information overload is key.

We live in a precarious age where nothing is certain and information is plentiful. When we couple this with a culture in which the violence of terrorism, the noise of advertising, and the overload of information compete for the constant attention of young adults, indeed the defining of the religious longings of young adults is no easy task.

To offer a healthy critique of the church, I raise the question of whether the church has been in touch with these elements of culture or if it has given young adults short shrift at times, seeking merely to move them into factions of the church based on providing a "spiritual quick fix" for the immediate longings of young adults, one that inevitably fails them in the long term.

3. Young adults, as a whole, are a generation of diversity.

There is no single "type" that can completely characterize either generation as a whole. Therefore, there are no sweeping generalizations in this book. This is both an asset and a hindrance for our ministerial approach because there is no "magic formula" that will attract all young adults into the life of the church. But to ignore this fact would be tragic. A targeted approach to one specific type of young person is a recipe for disaster in ministering to the needs of many.

Nonetheless, Millennials have a different generational identity than Gen Xers. The term *generational identity* refers simply to their viewpoint; that is:

1. how they see the world; and

2. how they derive meaning from that world to make sense of their own existence and the existence (or nonexistence) of God.

At this time of transition in American culture, it is not surprising that most Millennial young adults are looking for something solid to base their lives on, while the majority of the more experienced Generation Xers tend to view the world in a more pluralistic and explorative manner. This is a broad stroke that can explain much about both generations, and yet it is not all there is to say about them. There are also areas in which both generations meet. What is it that both generations truly long for? What can the church offer to both age groups for mutual benefit? Furthermore, for those who are already engaged in the church, what practices, rituals, and ministry programs attracted them initially, and have those practices served their long-term needs?

For the past five years I have worked within the Catholic Church alongside my colleagues (specifically, the Paulist Fathers, the Jesuits of the Chicago province, and ministry professionals, both lay and clerical, from all segments of the country) in attempting to serve the needs of young adults (defined, in terms of the ministerial distinctions in the Catholic Church, as those between the ages of eighteen and thirty-nine, both married and single). My work has led me to discover a great many things about the identity, longings, beliefs, affiliations, and vocational pursuits of this demographic. This book attempts to share my discoveries about young adults at the turn of the new millennium and also provide some suggestions for a ministerial approach within the Catholic Church for those who have the opportunity to minister to and with young adults at this time.

As a first step, I examine how we can define young adults of each generation. Simply stated, what are the differences and cross-over patterns in both demographics? I have collected knowledge on the longings of those in their twenties and thirties from many colleagues and authors who have explored this segment of society in their scholarly works. Sharon Parks, Father Brett Hoover, CSP, Father James Bacik, Mary Anne Reese, Thomas Beaudoin, Dean Hoge, Jackson Carroll and Wade Clark Roof, and Colleen Carroll Campbell have all contributed in many ways to my thoughts on this generation. I am indebted to all of them for their honest scholarship; and to those I know personally, I would like to say that I appreciate the time you have taken in mentoring me.

In the first chapter I attempt to give a broad landscape of young adult life. I also discuss the chasm between young adults in their thirties (roughly Gen Xers) and those younger than thirty (Millennials). An important element of the first chapter is a look at those young adults that we do not often see in church circles, the *unchurched*, for lack of a better term. I hope to provide a broad answer to the question *Who are young adults?* but not an overly simplistic one. And I have tried to draw a landscape from which we can launch a ministry.

The second chapter deals with what is working well in young adult ministry across the United States. My office's ministerial outreach contributes many of my thoughts, along with my work with colleagues in the National Catholic Young Adult Ministry Association and the United States Conference of Catholic Bishops. I have also used anecdotal sociological data gathered from Dean Hoge's study of young adult Catholics, Colleen Carroll Campbell's work on the group she calls "the new faithful," and the ministry of the Archdiocese of Chicago, where Father John Cusick and Katherine DeVries have been leaders in young adult ministry for over twenty-five years.

Chapters 3 and 4 are checkpoints. I interviewed twelve young adults (six Millennials, six Gen Xers) about their experience of how the church has reached out to them (or failed to reach them) over the course of their young adult lives. What has fed them? What has aggravated them? Do their longings correspond to the characterizations that I have set forth in earlier chapters? In other words, these young adults are simply the proof of the pudding.

Care has been taken to provide a wide ministerial range of young adults who have been active in both so-called liberal and conservative ministry experiences. These classifications are two terms that many people claim no longer apply to young adults in the church. I think there is some truth to that, but it would be premature to dismiss these labels. I also have interviewed two nonpracticing or minimally practicing Catholics (one Gen X, one Millennial) in addition to the others, for additional balance.

Based on all of the information gathered in the first three chapters, the remainder of the book is a suggestion.

One of the church's biggest drawing cards is the experience of World Youth Day. While in the United States we often think of this as an event for teens, the event itself is one to which all young adults are invited. In Chapter 5, I look at the good points and bad points of the World Youth Day experience through a young adult lens. Then hallmarks are provided for young adult ministry based on both the longings of the culture and how young adults have responded to our successful ministry efforts.

The first touchstone deals with the basics of a ministerial approach to young adults. Much of this is based on elements of Karl Rahner's anthropology and theology. This is addressed in chapter 6.

Chapter 7 offers a specific approach for starting ministry from the ground up. How do you recruit and find young adults? How do you continue to keep a young adult ministry fresh and exciting?

Chapter 8 is filled with unique resources. Some of the better Internet resources and other media methods that have engaged young adults are offered. Also, how to use the Internet in ministry and how to avoid misusing it are considered. Resources from my ministry with BustedHalo.com and others that my office has modeled will be primary here, but I also borrow segments from programs from all over the country. A brief section is offered on professional organizations, for those interested in young adult ministry.

This book serves not only to evaluate some of the current practices of the church in reaching out to young adults but also to highlight the best of what the church's ministry and church tradition have already offered. Dare I say that often the church's position is given short shrift in the general public and even in ministerial circles, much to the detriment of young adult ministry and the church itself.

The church can indeed engage young people in a way that brings them to make sense and order of a chaotic world. Most of all, it can preach the radical message of love to this generation. This book highlights the opportunities that we have to engage a culture and look at the practices that will serve the needs of the church for ages to come. It defines an approach to ministry that can ensure the church of both a vibrant present and future.

I hope you will rise to the challenge of young adult ministry with me. Know that the spirit is indeed with us on our journey.

PART I
Who Are Young Adults?

CHAPTER 1

IDENTIFYING YOUNG ADULTS

Would You Know a Young Adult If You Fell over One in the Aisle?

All ministers would like to be able to place the words "young adult ministry" into Google and let it spit out hundreds of links that point them to the silver key to ministering to this age. In today's culture this is a logical step for most, especially the young who try to minister to this age. Young adults often take the same measures when looking for a church (which yields 178,000,000 results), God (170,000,000 results), or Jesus Christ (27,900,000).

With this in mind, I would like to steer discussion on ministry not with a look inward to the church's ecclesiology and theology but rather with a look outward to American culture, the context in which young adults live their everyday lives. Sociologists Jackson W. Carroll and Wade Clark Roof state that "a generation's identity is, to a considerable extent, a narrative construct as people age and look back upon and interpret their experiences."[1] What are the stories (or narratives) of the two generations of young adults with whom we are concerned?

While attending a symposium at the University of Notre Dame, I was seated next to a group of fifty-something religious professionals. Their concern was that young adults were growing more conservative in their theology simply because they wanted to do eucharistic adoration often and were not terribly involved in the social justice aspects of the church's teaching. Their well-meaning concern was valid; however, it was horribly misguided. Young adults are not, by and large, looking for something more "conservative"; rather, they often seek a theology that is more contemplative and even more demanding of them. A simple look at American culture provides us with some answers and a context in which to view young adults.

In a world full of noise and images constantly vying for young adults' attention, is it surprising that young adults from both the Millennial and Gen X camps seek the quiet of contemplation in practices such as Taizé prayer or eucharistic adoration? Mystery in liturgy is something that both camps often look for. For the Millennials, especially, the world is filled with uncertainty. In talking with members of the Millennial generation, they tend to point to the major historical events that have marked their lives thus far: 9/11, the Columbine disaster, the Indian tsunami, Hurricane Katrina, the Virginia Tech Massacre. As they construct the meaning of their stories, they recall the moments when terrorists flew planes into buildings, high school students shot their colleagues at random, and water took the lives and homes of entire cities. Is it any wonder that young adults search for things that provide them with opportunities for contemplation and certainty? In a world where life seems very fleeting, young adults search for things they can depend on, things that have stood the test of time, things they regard as true, and things that are greater than themselves.

Roof and Carroll also note that the same is true about the generation known as Pre-Boomers. My parents, who were both born in 1928, are members of this generation. They too were affected by historical events: the Great Depression and the horror of World War II. Their Jewish friends would include the Holocaust as a life-forming event as well. Both Pope John Paul II and Pope Benedict XVI fall into this age group, and it is no surprise that the horror of the Holocaust is one event that has affected their entire worldview. Pope Benedict said, "At Auschwitz-Birkenau, humanity walked through 'a valley of darkness.'" Is it any wonder that young adults have profound respect for both men? In a sense, they all speak the same language, albeit at different points in history.

By the same token, Baby Boomers (those over the age of forty) responded to the events of Vietnam and Kent State in a different, dramatic fashion, eschewing authority for government's abusing power and holding institutions to a higher standard for their failures. We will see the trickle-down effects of this on Gen Xers, who also tend to be suspicious of authority and institutions, although generally in a different and sometimes a more apathetic way.

In all, these experiences drew people together. They formed bonds as they experienced the terror of war, the struggle of poverty, and especially for the recent Millennial group, the terror of uncertainty in a world filled with unconscionable and irrational violence. However, when I look at my own generation, Generation X, I cannot summon a single event historically that united us as a tight-knit community during our early adult formation. Carroll and Roof also note that "only 31 percent of Generation Xers feel they belong to a distinctive generation."[2] When I ask my friends about this phenomenon they struggle to name a single world event that had a life-changing effect on the way they view the world. Some mention the Iranian hostage crisis, Tiananmen Square, the Berlin Wall falling, but all of them also note that they didn't live in fear after these moments, nor did community form strongly around these events, even if they were united around the cause. I often classify Gen Xers as too young for Vietnam and Watergate and too old for the effects of terrorism to take total hold of their worldview.

What does this mean for us as ministers in the Catholic Church? Most often I hear those who minister with Millennial young adults state that they "don't want to talk about how God (or a spiritual experience) makes them feel. Rather, they want answers that are straightforward." Inversely, those who meet with Gen Xers often state that they will give their lives in service but never connect that experience with a sense of religious conviction. In fact, some eschew Sunday Mass in favor of working at a soup kitchen as their Sunday ritual.

We indeed have a young adult generation gap. Undoubtedly, the major influence here is their experience of world events. That has formed the Millennials' longing for certainty and for a God who orders everything and makes sense of their world. Gen Xers, meanwhile, may suffer from a lack of meaning in the recent experiences of violence, terrorism, and natural disasters, but they respond differently, grasping tightly communal and nurturing relationships for security rather than expressing an intellectual need for certitude.

Differences in Family Experiences

Here is a second divide between Gen X and Millennial young adults. Generation X "felt the pain of family disruption with 45 percent of them being in a family that experienced either divorce or separation or were raised by single parents."[3] Second, Gen Xers were far more likely to be raised by parents who were both working. Because of the lack of emotional support from their parents they are most likely to express those feelings of loss; therefore, Generation X longs for community more than any other generation. Roof and Carroll note:

> Because they have been deprived in stable primary relationships, many do look to cultivate close personal ties within a religious community. Identity becomes

deeply rooted with a social network. On occasion, within the Catholic community sects that supported the idea of a communal focus during liturgy, strong retreat programs that built unity and deep friendships, and opportunities to bring people together in service to others usually turned out to garner more support from the members of Generation X.[4]

I know from my own personal experience that those programs on the Fordham campus that worked well were those of retreat ministry and community service. If the campus ministry sponsored a program entitled "The Truths of the Catholic Faith," it would garner few attendees. Experience is at the crux of Generation X's meaning-making mechanism. The friends I made in college through campus ministry and service programs were like a family (and in some ways they still are). The bonds holding us together came from the experience of going through a retreat where we talked about our deepest feelings and thoughts, or a service project where we experienced the poorest of the poor in Appalachia or Nicaragua. Our bonds did not rest merely upon our Catholic faith or even our personal beliefs. Rather, they formed because we shared an experience together that helped us firm up our worldview. My friend Graham once remarked that our retreat was so wonderful because "nobody was right or wrong. We simply were together sharing an experience of one another, understanding where we were all coming from in terms of faith and being OK in the midst of our uncertainty about life and the future. We knew this was a holy moment and Jesus was right there among us."

The authority that the church had for my college classmates was only as strong as the experience of faith it could provide for us. A good example was my friend Dusty, who was a staunch atheist. He became friends with the priest in his dorm where he served as a resident assistant, and the combination of this priest's friendliness and his friends' encouragement led him to attend a retreat with campus ministry that all of his friends raved about. Upon his return he said: "Well…many of you know that this was kind of God's last shot with me. I've never believed in God, mostly because I have never had an experience of God that I thought was trustworthy. Let's just say that this weekend God won a few battles with me." Experience has indeed proven to be the best teacher for Generation X.

Millennial young adults, on the other hand, have grown up as the most watched-over generation in history. They often accept authority figures as trustworthy and believe that rules are good things and that one should follow them (for example, they have never ridden a bicycle without a helmet). When Millennials go to church, they respond to preaching that instructs them on how to behave more than how to believe. They want quick answers that can be immediately integrated into their lives.

Millennials also see church as a way to "clear the cobwebs out of their brain." They need to find relief both from the saturation of the media and the competition of the rat race. They also hope to meet likeminded members of the opposite sex in church, because most often, they find comfort in a homogeneous community. In short, the Millennial church believes that there has to be more to life than the sum of our experiences— mostly because a good number of those experiences are dreadful and horrifying.

Generation Xers and Baby Boomers wanted religion that challenged them spiritually to become more involved in the lives of one another and their community. They wanted to care more and wanted people who would be there for them. The authority figures in their lives, from parents to politicians, had proved to be suspect, and therefore the institutional church also lacked relevance in their lives. More often than not, during Gen Xers' time of transition from teenagers to young adults the

Catholic Church ignored them or criticized them. The question they most respond to is Who will be there for me?

Millennials often seek the reverse of Generation Xers in church. They don't want church to be the place where community comes together but rather the place where quiet mystery serves them well. Because of the strong supervision that members of this generation had, they intuitively sense that they are unconditionally loved, but they also look for ways to prove that love on an intellectual plane. It is not enough for them to know that they are loved; they need to prove their worthiness of that love through solid service to the community, unwavering loyalty to a religious tradition, repentance, and in the Catholic sense, a rigid adherence to the laws of the church as stated in the catechism. They seek to answer the question, Why am I worthy of love?

For the unchurched Millennials, however, religion may be less threatening than it was for their Gen X counterparts, who found religion to be for crackpots and weak-minded people. They, however, seem to be just as threatened by institutions and more jaded than most of those who adhere to tradition. For some, nihilism has surfaced as an alternative, because without a religious tradition to help them make sense of the world, the world becomes a vast wasteland; the murderer who massacred his fellow students at Virginia Tech is an extreme example of this. (Note that many in this group come from poorer homes, divorced households, and/or abusive relationships and are exceptions to the rule. They were not as cared for as a typical Millennial was in a home that regarded family as paramount.)

Converging Patterns of Mystery

Whether it is communal or intellectual, both groups have some appreciation of the mystical sense of the divine; indeed, that is where the groups converge. The small difference is that Gen Xers tend to be able to see that experience of mystery in intimate relationships while Millennials have a more individualistic piety that only transfers itself to the communal life in an activity in which religious tenets are being displayed. In short, the Millennials will participate in communal activities when matters of individual salvation are discussed or where strong symbols of a specific religiosity are present. Without these elements, it is simply a waste of their time. Harvard Professor Harvey Cox makes a great point in reference to his students, in essence saying that they realize that they are never going to know everything that others think they should know.[5] Time is limited. There are things to do. Competition is fierce. In religious experience they mostly want to be assured that a ritual or experience of faith is filled with mystery and going to be worth their time. One young adult recently mentioned to me: "If it's not something that I can't find anywhere else and it's not going to help me get to heaven, then why bother?"

Testing Truth

In the minds of young adults, truths need to be validated by experience, whether communal or intellectual. For Gen Xers, the tenets of the faith are tested through critical reasoning, where every theory is fair game for scrutiny. For the Millennials, the burden of proof does not fall upon authority but rather upon whether they can "measure up" and prove themselves worthy of the centuries-old tradition that they adhere to.

There is wisdom in both groups. Generation X does not allow for a blind faith that is tantamount to an unthinking piety, and while the Millennial "new faithful" occasionally fall into that trap, they also epitomize the beauty of Catholic tradition by their unwavering adherence and their ability to show that they can live up to the high standards that the church sets for all of us.

Colleen Carroll states that young adults are further defined by "a belief in absolute truth and objective standards of morality."[6] She claims that young adults identify with conservative traditions like Opus Dei or Regnum Christi rather than groups focused on social justice, like Pax Christi. While she does not specify, I believe Carroll is describing Millennial young adults more than any other demographic. I also believe she is definitely onto something here. Young adults, especially Millennials, are certainly looking for something rock solid in which they can place their faith. The church needs to go a step further than noticing this trend and reacting to it in a ministerial way. We need to look at why they want this rock-solid faith in their lives. Until we do this, we cannot address their longing for certainty holistically or even appropriately. Most often ministers act as the culture does, giving young adults a quick-fix spiritual approach. This provides some instant gratification, which young adults respond to, but it also reduces God to Santa Claus, doling out spiritual ritual that provides comfort but may in fact be harmful to contemplation and spiritual integration. Furthermore, what happens when God doesn't become manifest in a bolt-of-lightning, "born-again" kind of moment? I have found that in that case most young adults run screaming away from the church, because they believe that it has failed them. The quick-fix ritual provides little for those outside of specific conservative Catholic communities, especially when we speak of those who are raised within environments of poverty where ambiguity is often commonplace and even somewhat comfortable.

In my pastoral experience I have been struck by the number of ministers who speak of young adults who are unwilling (or perhaps unable) to express their spiritual longings and their feelings in favor of simply knowing "the law." Many people report that the striking difference between Gen Xers and Millennials is that Gen Xers might not be able to articulate facts surrounding their tradition but they can indeed articulate their spiritual experiences rather well. Millennials often can articulate their beliefs well but have no idea how they came to believe a particular tenet of the faith or even why the tradition espouses it. They simply adhere to the church's teaching without much thought as to why they are doing so. My own pastoral experience has revealed to me (and this becomes evident in the later interviews) that people need more than simple truth statements. They need to be mentored in the navigation of an ambiguous world. When rigid truth claims become difficult to follow or when life comes into conflict with their sense of the way the world works, young adults need spiritual mentors, not judgmental zealots who simply point to the letter of the law. Carroll's work is paramount to this discussion. Her identification of young adults who long for certainty and who resort to a rigid orthodoxy to satisfy their longing for truth is absolutely true. My challenge to those who have experienced much success in garnering those defined as the new faithful to their parish or ministry is that giving them simple truth claims and catechism sound bytes to adhere to is simply an incomplete approach in the long term. Those that minister to the new faithful simply by telling them that they need to align themselves strongly with a conservative tradition in the church cater to young adults' tendency to treat religion like the Google search engine: They put a problem in and expect an immediate answer. God is not quite that simple. These ministers are ignoring the larger faith longings of young adults and have played into American culture's quick-fix mentality. Young adults need to place the sound bytes of Catholic tradition into their present context as well as the church's historical context in order to grasp the spirit of the law as well as the letter of it. They need strong mentors who will minister with them with much care and provide more than easy memorization or rigid adherence. When the truths of religious faith butt up against the ambiguities of life itself, especially life within American culture, young adults need to set critical reasoning skills alongside their strong adherence to a faith tradition in order to navigate through that ambiguity and through the dark nights of the soul that we all experience. When doubt sets in, the catechism will only serve young adults as a reference, not as a mentor. Who stands with the young adult who finds herself pregnant or seeking divorce from an abusive husband? Who is there for young adults, with not only a confessional stole at the ready but a commitment to journey with them through their problems and their brokenness? Especially now, as the shortage of priests in the United States increases, a lay minister's paramount responsibility will lie here. We cannot simply throw answers at young adults. Rather, we need to be mentors, servants to those in need of ministerial guidance.

Classifying the Diversity of Young Adults

While there are no sweeping generalities that apply to these two groups, there is a plurality of classifications that define different factions of both generations. At a recent symposium at the University of Notre Dame, Father Jim Bacik presented a paper on the spirituality of the Millennial generation as he has come to experience them in his work as a campus minister at the University of Toledo. Bacik provided a sampling of seven different types of spiritual identities that young adults identify with. Mary Anne Reese provided a similar viewpoint in *America* magazine but extended the categories to both Millennial and Generation X young adults. It is the combination of these identifications that I use to define young adults. They include the following:

Eclipsed

These are young adults who show no interest in either spiritual or religious matters. They have "better things to do." These young adults show little interest in ritual and perhaps do not even pray. A typical example is a young adult Catholic who struggles to make ends meet and works an extra shift on Sunday rather than attending Sunday Mass, or the young adult family that finds it too much of a bother to get the children dressed for 10 o'clock Mass when they could spend quality time in their pajamas playing at home.

The mistake that many religious professionals make in ministering to these people is that they assume these particular young adults have no spiritual experience because at face value they seem to be disinterested in all things spiritual. However, a deeper look shows that they merely have "eclipsed" faith. There is no time for church or an intentional faith experience because of the demands of a busy culture and the irrelevance of religious institutions, which they see evidenced by the sex-abuse scandals of the Catholic Church, or even the hypocritical nature of the modern televangelist.

While these eclipsed young adults may in fact have felt the presence of the divine in their everyday experience, most often they may not articulate this by using religious language or even referring to a conscious experience of God. Their feeling is often described as "unbelievable" or "indescribable" or "being moved" to a sense of awe. They report these profound experiences most often while communing with nature, sitting in silence, witnessing the birth of a baby, or conversing deeply with friends and mentors. They experience the "other" in these nontraditional ways (read: outside of the church doors and traditional ritual), but they seemingly have come away with the same inclinations about the mysterious as those of us who have felt that same presence during a religious ritual or while praying traditional prayers.

A minority may also have direct experiential reasons for holding faith in disregard. A poor faith formation that reinforced immaturity (for example, using religion as a means of control by a parent or a cleric), an experience of clergy that was either abusive or hurtful, or even boring liturgical Sundays can make the faith feel irrelevant in the real world for some. For the few that have been abused, reconciliation does not seem possible in their minds, and their need to remain psychologically stable as a result of the abuse eclipses their need for spirituality. Needless to say, this is a tragedy that the church should place in paramount importance.

For the remaining eclipsed Catholics, many hope that maturity and life experience will bring them back into the fold of active Catholicism. However, this may not to be the case. William Dinges and others write: "Growing older by itself has no overall effect in pushing basic values one direction or another. We should not expect that today's young people will come to resemble today's older adults when they mature."[7] I have found young adulthood, for most, to be a time of transition, when core values are not formed but are reformed (a subject I return to later). People enter young adulthood with a very stable although untested worldview. They have come to know much about the world they live in through their teenage years and have formed a basic set of values. During young adulthood these values are challenged, and new ideas place old thoughts at peril. Ideas need to change when met with new ones that make sense or the young adult will face an unsure and anxious future. Once ideas are reformed, very little change in those values will occur beyond this period of growth unless trauma or some other serious life event alters that worldview further. The hope for future reconciliation with the church without a solid plan seems somewhat severe as a panacea, yet it does leave us some room for examination.

Several of these eclipsed young adults will indeed return to the church for a baptism or a funeral or in smaller numbers for a wedding, and this provides an opportunity for ministers to take advantage of such "moments of return." (This practice will be considered in chapter 2.) Therefore, ministers to young adults need to pay careful attention not only to the times they choose to evangelize intentionally to young adults but also to the times when "eclipsed" young adults are present for ordinary liturgical celebrations and encounters in the parish.

Private

Not far removed from the eclipsed Catholic is the private Catholic. This young adult finds little use for outward display or public ritual but instead pursues spiritual goals on his or her own, albeit in an intentional manner. Such private Catholics may read religious books, swim in the ocean, or spend time praying privately. While spirituality is perhaps part of their everyday experience, public expression is not. My friend Sarah, a nonpracticing Catholic, is a good example. She feels closest to God when bodysurfing in the Pacific Ocean, the waves taking her vulnerable body out with the tide. Yet she does not participate in a Sunday Mass ritual. Her experience is nonetheless a spiritual one, and she never misses an opportunity to hit the waves.

Perhaps the deep suspicion of institutions that Gen Xers hold leads to this type of private faith. Private prayer is more relevant to them than Mass on Sunday (or any other public faith expression, for that matter) because most often they have not been affected by the church (most people would inaccurately report that young adults have been disaffected or alienated by the church structures). Their lives are often marked by one or both of the following experiences that provide a death knell for the faith of Gen Xers and Millennials: a boring or staid experience of church ritual coupled with a lack of social interaction and/or a liturgical church experience that lacks quiet mystery and opportunity for contemplation in favor of social banter. In short, liturgy that provides a strong opportunity for contemplation and mystery in both preaching and ritual as well as a strong sense of welcome and hospitality that does not detract from the mystical aspects of ritual is what is called for. It is my opinion that some of these private young adults are simply introverted and their experience of God, like other matters, remains concealed. Because Gen Xers were often ignored in favor of a parental choice to put career ahead of family, they spent a majority of their time alone. Perhaps it was in this time when they formed a rich spirituality, realizing that God is their sole provider, all that they can count on, because simply put, there was nobody around to depend on, talk to, or with whom to commune. This can result in favoring a spirituality of privacy as well.

The Millennials long for escape from this privacy and seek a place where they can be unashamed to be Catholic. They want to prove their worthiness of their faith but may not have the courage or the spiritual self-esteem to do so and end up wallowing in self-pity. In chapter 2 we look at some young adult ministry programs that are bringing Millennial young adults into the forefront of Catholic identity.

Ecumenical

While a growing number of young adults simply assume that the divisions among Christians make no sense and younger Catholics note that ecumenism is inherent in their culture, sporting a variety of friends of different religions, questions of salvation still loom large, especially among Millennial young adults. On BustedHalo.com (the Web site that I cofounded with Fr. Brett Hoover, CSP, in 2001), the most oft-asked question by young adults is about interfaith marriage. Most of the time, it is a Catholic asking if "it's allowed" for Catholics to marry non-

Catholics, and most often the question comes from someone under the age of twenty-seven. Second, BustedHalo often gets asked about questions of salvation directly. "Is my Jewish friend going to hell?" was a recent question that was e-mailed to me. A growing number of neoconservative young adults that I have encountered in my work believe that their faith is the only true faith, and they cast judgment on others in kind. Many spiritual seekers report that questioning faith is often unwelcome in various Catholic young adult groups. Even those of a more progressive bent still fret about ecumenical differences within families and seem to suffer from a "not in my neighborhood" mentality in regard to ecumenism. So while many young adults are filled with ecumenical zeal and many believe that one religion just might be as good as another, it is important to note that many of the younger set young adults look for something more separatist, something that convinces them that they are "right," "special," or "saved." In broader terms, however, especially among the unchurched, the majority of young adults do indeed have a strong sense of ecumenical fervor. They don't have any issues with interfaith marriage but, at the same time, spirituality is important to them in choosing a partner, and they tend to look for someone who at minimum holds the same basic moral beliefs as they do (ethically, at least) despite denominational differences. Often a strong ecumenical catechesis is welcomed among all groups to make clear what the differences between the various faiths are and why divisions still exist. Culturally, many people are more accepting of religious freedom; however with the rise of fundamentalist Islam and the terrorist groups that co-opt that faith, many have become more rigid and unwavering in their approach to other religions.

Evangelical

Some young adults within the church flock to praise and worship services filled with vibrant music and hold an emotive sense of prayer in high regard. They hope to use all their senses in prayer. Father Bacik reported at Notre Dame that "a few are really fundamentalists, who act aggressively in preserving their Catholic heritage from the threats of the contemporary world and the reforms of Vatican II, which appear to them as excessive and dangerous."[8]

We should be cautious of an unthinking piety and a false intellectualism among this group of fundamentalist Catholics. Their emotive sense of prayer, while important, also limits our aspect of transcendence and mystery, placing God only in the experience of our senses. At the same time, we recall that it is in our senses that we experience all that we do and are. It is a necessary element of being human. It would justifiably be correct then to use sense experience as a mediator to get to transcendence. The problem is that many young adults stop their spiritual searching with the experience of sensuality. The categorical replaces the transcendent in such a way that it blocks the opportunity for transcendent experience.

Not surprisingly, these young adults are often looking for something to fill the hole that is missing in their lives. Sometimes the sensual experiences they find in drug abuse or sexuality is a cheap substitute for what is missing in a deep faith life. Indeed, the converse is also true; an evangelical faith can substitute for experiences of heightened sensuality. In many ways this can be a good thing, but in certain cases it can be another cheap sensual substitute, providing only a Google-like sensual quick fix. I have found that many young adults in recovery from addictions often rely on this type of evangelical faith, and for them this might be a very good and viable option. More often, however, the remainder of evangelical young adults find a sense of holiness in simple emotive prayer and ritual experiences like the "Life Teen" Masses (which young adults long past the teenage demographic still attend), with vibrant Christian rock music, emotional preaching, and rigid commitment to the group. While the style of liturgy is vibrant and often first-rate, the cultlike principles of emotional manipulation may similarly be at play. It is mere sensual experience that results in a feel-good spirituality. These experiences don't make room for the proverbial dark night of the soul or a sense of quiet contemplation. As an example, I point to a young woman who turned her life completely over to God after years of a horrible addiction. She threw herself headlong into praying with all her senses at Mass. If she didn't attend Mass she missed the experience greatly. But outside of the ritual experience, she struggled, especially as the memory of that week's ritual faded. Mass became another fix. While one could be addicted to worse things, to be able to stand healthy and integrated without having to have some kind of sensual experience as a constant companion is certainly a preferable option.

Second, and most threatening to our young adult culture, is the experience of Catholic fundamentalism. Unlike Protestant fundamentalism, where the Bible is the literal word of God, in Catholic fundamentalist circles the Bible is replaced with the *Catechism of the Catholic Church*, which is rigidly viewed as the truth to which we all must conform. Communities with attitudes of Catholic fundamentalism not only polarize those who come into contact with them in casual conversation, they also "outside" those in disagreement, or those who attempt to more carefully reconstruct a possibly stronger Catholic position by challenging what is presently considered to be flawed in the catechism in their view (such as viewpoints on homosexuality, the necessity of war, and the role of women and the laity in liturgy)—or perhaps a viewpoint given from the hierarchy. Because young adults of an evangelical nature are looking for something that is solid to grasp onto during this time of transition, many of these young adults will come to the forefront of ministry experience with expectations of finding a religion that is universally true. The pluralistic world often challenges this worldview, as do the crushing forces of ambiguity, or alternative viewpoints that seem to make sense. It is here most often that we find young adults (especially Millennial young adults) in a spiritual crisis with a catechism in their hands but no spiritual mentors to help them put the wisdom of the catechism in context.

Many evangelical young adults clearly find a healthy sense of the transcendent in an emotive experience that they are able to translate into a solid experience of faith. They are neither polarizing nor rigid, and they often have a healthy outlook toward mentoring teens and other young adults. For the most part, they become solid leaders in ritual, prayer groups, retreats, and ministries in the church. Clerics would be wise to try to tap into the healthy people in this group to charge up their ministry or parish and give it new life.

Sacramental

Some active churchgoing young adults are in tune with the rhythms of the liturgy and find joy in the sacraments that the church offers. They may even have a sense of the sacramental nature of the whole world, seeing the spirit of God imbued in all of nature's wonder. It is in the traditional sacramental moments that many of these people are intent on meeting the Lord working in their lives. They are a prayerful people who make time for ritual and engage in the experience joyfully. They see great value in the traditional practices that the church offers and oftentimes are abhorred by changes in these practices. Many are colloquially called "smells and bells" Catholics and are much like the evangelical Catholics we described who use all their senses in prayer. Similarly, sacramental young adults find that they too are moved by liturgy. It is often only during liturgical events that they find spiritual experience in their lives, longing for them all week long (or until the next opportunity presents itself in things like a Wednesday night eucharistic adoration service, or prayer group, or Taizé singing). This group is a significant minority and virtually nonexistent in the unchurched young adult demographic, falling in direct opposition to the eclipsed young adult demographic.

Prophetic

These are the young adults who live out the practice of their faith by going against the grain of the status quo. They are active in service projects with and for the poor. They work for peace in organizations like Pax Christi and Bread for the World. They run soup kitchens and shelters for the homeless and people with AIDS. They seek the Catholic tradition through Catholic Social Teaching (CST) when it is offered to them; unfortunately for many "service seekers," it is still the church's best-kept secret. They openly see value in serving the needs of others and may even link that value to recalling the "golden rule" that Christ points out in the gospel. However, they most often do not link social justice with the traditions of their Catholic denomination—even if the practices are basic tenets of the faith. Jesus is often a conscious model for these folks, but they don't explore that sense of Christianity beyond a simple sense of service. They simply "do what Jesus would do." Good works are enough. However, a small minority of this group do see that justice is uniquely linked with Catholicism, and they bring that zeal into parish communities and parish service programs. They form social ministry programs, run parish soup kitchens, and even form mission trips to foreign countries. They are inspirational to older parishioners and often find themselves being asked to take on parish leadership roles in the community. Many Gen Xers and unchurched Catholics who are culturally Catholic prefer their experience of direct service to our Sunday ritual Mass experience. The communal spirit of prayer gives way to the feeling they get in doing good works. The Millennial young adults who are prophetic often find their prophetic call as the result of examining the documents of the church's teachings in the catechism and in CST. Most often Millennial young adults are involved in campaigns for life issues like abortion and birth control; however, a growing number of them are beginning to work in the inner city with the poor, especially in the area of education.

Communal

These are the extroverts of the church. They need to pray but they never pray alone. They have a great regard for social ministry groups, faith sharing, and retreats. They usually seek like-minded Catholics in these activities.

Like the evangelicals, this group also needs to be on guard for an "unthinking piety": Is faith only for the times when I get together with my friends? Or when I'm on retreat? We are human beings and not human doings. The danger of the communal is to fall into the trap of living an unexamined life. These young adults may never critically scrutinize their own lives in the stillness of their heart, preferring to jump into a new group or see themselves only in the light of another. They tend to join several groups and participate in many activities and make many friends. Some fall prey to superficiality, seeking loose relationships that keep others at a distance. On the positive side, communal young adults are often the backbone of many leadership efforts in parish ministry with young adults. They have the gifts of hospitality and communication and are often able to mobilize and inspire people in ways that others cannot. They also often unconsciously have Jesus as their model. Jesus is the man who was accused of eating and drinking too much with his friends, who valued others so much that he felt it was necessary to spend much of his time with them. The best examples in this group get to know others well and care for the needs of their community intimately. They are often inspiring people who give much of themselves to others. Good examples of communal young adults are those in my New York City parish who helped serve the needs of one of their parishioners who lost a spouse after September 11.

Conclusion

Mary Anne Reese's and Father James Bacik's classifications of young adults are certainly the wide-ranging lens that I will refer to in these classifications in the remainder of the book. While Colleen Carroll has significant things to add to this conversation, I will keep her thoughts ancillary to Bacik's and Reese's main thesis in our process of defining young adults. The bottom line here is that Bacik and Reese are wise enough to know that young adults are unidentifiable as a whole, and a piecemeal approach will serve us better in looking at how we approach them from a ministerial sense. In the following chapter I will look at what is working in the Catholic Church in young adult ministry and then explore typical young adult ministerial experience. We will need to keep not only these identifications of young adults in mind but also Jackson Carroll's and Wayne Roof's valuable generational trends that I believe can further help us define what the church will need to do in order to continue to attract young adults to the church.

CHAPTER 2

WHAT'S WORKING WELL IN YOUNG ADULT MINISTRY?

Ministry Superstars of the Modern Age

Google teaches us a few things. First, it is the primary place that young people look for anything. Second, if you don't search, you don't find. Jesus himself cautioned his followers to "seek and you shall find." It is from this type of motto that those who are ministering well to young adults have derived their lessons.

How has the church ministered recently to young adults? The answer to that question for the past twenty-five years has been, most often, not at all. The traditional parish model employed by the Catholic Church tends to as a whole not know what to do about this group. Traditional parish ministry is aimed at families, teens, and the elderly as a primary means of out-reach. This parish experience is still the main experience that most people will have with a church if they have one at all. Just as all politics is local, all "church" is local.

Parishes typically having a connection with a grammar school or high school are only engaged with young adults who have school-age children. Many single young adults who have recently left their campus ministry parish (or their high school teen ministry) and have now either returned to their hometown or gone to a new environment where they have moved since graduation tend to be ignored. Even among the married young adults the focus in these cases is most often on their child and not on a ministerial outreach or the spiritual longings and needs of the parents.

Instead of outreach to a highly mobile and hard-to-reach generation, many pastors have given up on this demographic group, hoping that they will return to liturgical practice and active parish involvement when they intend to marry, need to baptize a child, or most important, when their child begins school (preferably the parish's Catholic school, and most especially in urban environments). They are happy to have the few Millennial or Gen X young adults who frequently work harder at parish ministries than the remainder of the parish does. In some cases these young adults revitalize the parish on their own. However, these young adults are often few in number with regard to parish life.

While "moments of return" to the church come at significant times in the life of the adult, the trend does not always correlate with a return to active religious practice, nor is it certain to lead to involvement in a local parish community. But most significantly, life events like marriage or baptism have also not coincided with a return of young adults to the church of their birth. Many young adults seek marriage outside Catholicism, even if they have no impediments to being married in the church. Still, the majority of people seeking marriage continue to identify themselves with Catholicism as their religion of choice. Sociologist and priest Andrew Greeley recently reported that "about a third of young Catholics, under thirty-five, neither of them married before, are presently not married in the Church. However, when asked, four out of five of them plan to raise their children Catholic!"[1]

Ministering to young adults is indeed a bit like trying to herd cats. We are talking about a diverse and mobile generation, one that wants things to happen instantaneously. Many are suspicious of institutions (especially those who have been outside the church for extended periods), and yet we are also talking about a generation that seeks spirituality possibly more than any other has in the past because of their uncertain future.

Taking the models of young adults proposed in the first chapter, I would like to examine some approaches taken in ministry that have been "succeeding." By using the word *success*, I am not advocating or promoting the use of any of these methods. I use the word as a modifier to point to the fact that these methods have garnered high numbers of attendees at the ministerial programs.

For Eclipsed Catholics: The Ministry of "Moments of Return"

While young adults are often "too busy for church," they do indeed make their way back into the church from time to time. It is these "moments of return" that Father John Cusick and Katherine DeVries of the Archdiocese of Chicago's Young Adult Ministry Office have turned into huge opportunities for both celebration and ministry. Cusick notes five clear-cut moments of return that the church can use as opportunity:

a) Marriage

Many marriages take place during the young adult period of life. Often it may appear that young adults are asked to jump through hoops in order to simply have their wedding ceremony in a given parish. One young adult told Cusick, "I called five churches today looking for a place to be married. Every one asked if I was registered. Not one even asked if I was Catholic! And no one even bothered to ask if I was in love!"[2] Cusick, a close colleague of mine, suggests that we have an opportunity to give young adults an experience of sacrament that they will find memorable and not compulsory. "We need to learn how to celebrate moments of return, how we can celebrate the most profound moment of love in these two young lives. I am always so honored to be asked to preside at these moments in people's lives. I firmly believe that giving them a wedding day and a good preparation experience means that they will look back fondly on our efforts and that will serve us better than trying to get them to sign on the dotted line and sending them a bunch of envelope packages."

Cusick also criticizes the approach of forcing young adults to register as a compulsory task in the marriage process. "They will do it our way if they are forced to, but they will also remember that. When the assembly gathers to be in communion with one another young adults will not feel in union with that assembly."

b) Baptism

The same holds true for baptism. One young adult couple I know asked to have their child baptized and were turned away simply because they were not members of the parish. Where did they end up? The Episcopal church down the street! Lesson learned? We need to worry less about registration and more about experience in a ministerial sense. If we give young adults an experience that they treasure and can hold dear, the chances that they return on at least an occasional basis are great. This is a generation used to getting things at the touch of a button. They can, and often do, vote with their feet when compulsory tasks are viewed as insignificant or unnecessary. Cusick argues that the more we require of people the less commitment we will get in return.

c) Moments of Sickness

Some young adults will either be faced with illness themselves or be engaged in the illness of a loved one, be it parent, grandparent, child, or spouse. How do hospital chaplains engage young adults in conversation during these moments? Do pastors who happen to hear of a young parishioner's illness pay them a visit just to chat and see how they are doing spiritually at this difficult time? When a young adult asks for prayers for their dying parent, do we ever add that we will also pray for them? Do we seek them out when we see them visiting relatives in hospitals or taking someone to the doctor's office?

d) Death

Funerals and wakes are also opportunities for pastoral engagement. Death, especially unexpected death, often shatters a young adult's world. When indeed do we have a better opportunity to speak with a young adult who needs us, to reach out and be present for him or her? We naturally need to be pastorally sensitive to personal and familial boundaries here, but an offer to talk and be present should always be made by a lay pastoral minister or priest in this situation. Young adults especially remember that someone took the time for them during this period of darkness. Often the death of a loved one is a critical time of reframing meaning for young people—a time when they can use guidance.

e) Personal Decision/Change of Life

Young adults will likely change careers, not merely jobs, three times in their lifetime. What goes into these personal lifestyle changes? What can we offer to people who are mired in the process of discerning choices? How do we advertise spiritual direction services or retreats for young adults? Do we give freely of our time when they seek our assistance, or do we push them away because we are too busy with other pastoral concerns?

All of these moments are crucial times in the lives of these young people that we can easily pay attention to as ministers.

Cusick adds, "They are moments of meaning and personal identity. These moments open young adults to the spiritual side of their lives." Father Cusick's passion for highlighting the "moment of return" is understandable; young adults have actively responded to this "moment" for more than two decades.

For Private Catholics: Video Divina and BustedHalo.com

Favoring a quiet introversion to communal worship, private young adults have been served well by a method of prayer developed by Tom Beaudoin, a professor of theology at Santa Clara University, which I call Video Divina. Beaudoin, also the author of the well-regarded book *Virtual Faith: The Irreverent Spiritual Quest of Generation X,* often touts pop culture as the "amniotic fluid in which young adults become familiar with themselves."[3] Beaudoin identifies the clear technological merging of faith with young adult spirituality and describes certain contextual aspects of young adulthood in which both Millennial and Generation X young adults comingle. Pop culture and media are clearly where most young adults find their news, entertain themselves, set trends, and make assumptions about the world. What they see virtually in images on a daily basis can speak to the way they form meaning in the everyday.

Thomas Beaudoin might go a bit overboard in his classifications of young adults in his book *Virtual Faith,* as he is a kind of hipster musician (Beaudoin plays in a rock band in addition to his teaching and writing), but he has identified clearly an aspect of what drives the private young adult demographic. This group finds their contemplation in listening to music or watching television or film, or even being alone in a nature scene. They do so not out of a sense of "coolness" or because they have a constant need for pop culture, but simply because it is a world that they have grown accustomed to, engaging their senses and their minds privately. Beaudoin suggests that we use this as an advantage for those who engage more readily with popular culture than with religiosity. For young adults, an episode of *The Simpsons* can be a religious moment. Beaudoin pointed this out at the 2004 Los Angeles Religious Education Conference as he described a group of his students who use the weekly *Simpsons* episodes each Sunday as a conduit to spiritual contemplation. He suggests that while his students gather collectively to discuss the spiritual themes of the show, most young adults do this solo. They watch music videos, listen to iPods, and view films with the aim of learning something about themselves, the world around them, and perhaps even God. Beaudoin gives his group intentional questions as a spiritual exercise to guide these meditative moments of immersion within popular culture.

I use this method in my retreat program as an opening ice-breaker, and it has delivered great results. (85 percent of the retreat attendees mentioned that it was a great way to get us in the spiritual flow of the weekend right away.) The method, in short, deals with taking a piece of popular culture (e.g., a music video, a film clip, a TV episode, etc.) and viewing it while considering the following questions:

- Where do you see yourself in the video?
- Where do you feel distant from the action?
- What speaks to you in the video most?
- What repulses you?
- Finally, where do you find God in the video and where is God seemingly absent?

Private young adults enjoy contemplation and mulling over their spiritual lives. They see no need to be in a church to concentrate on their relationship with God. They, like Ignatius of

Loyola, can easily see "God in all things," but prefer to do so in solitude rather than in communal settings. Beaudoin suggests that we, as ministers, can use this generality to provide a profound opportunity to merge the sacred with the secular.

The same can be said for those of us who do Web ministry. BustedHalo.com attempts to connect young adults with the best prayerful Web sites in its "How to pray" section. Web sites like the Irish Jesuits' www.sacredspace.ie provide a quick version of doing the Ignatian Examen, while www.rejesus.com provides a more multimedia experience, linking video and art with voice-over meditations. The Web magazine section of BustedHalo.com gives young people one new article a day and speaks about merging everyday experience with an experience of spirituality. All of this can be done from the privacy of your desktop computer.

Naturally, the danger here always falls with favoring this virtual experience for the actual experience of communal prayer. I would argue that not to use this familiar medium with private young adults is to be nonexistent to them. Private young adults will remain private if not engaged in some way. Often young adults use search engines like Google to find out the best offerings in a variety of subjects. They also use it to find a church, spiritual information, and Catholic tradition. To use a familiar medium to attract them to the contemplation and reflection the church offers may in fact be the only way to get this group to think about "church" at all and link it to their nonecclesial sense of faith. To not have a Web presence is to become invisible to this generation.

For Ecumenical Catholics: The Question Box

Increasingly, interfaith and ecumenical issues come up in the lives of young adults, and asking questions of ministers usually takes center stage when they do. An approach that we have used that has drawn huge numbers to events and retreats we have sponsored is called "The Question Box." In this forum we ask people to write a question that may be concerning them in regard to what the church teaches on a given subject. What most often happens is a discussion on what other faiths have to say about a particular issue, as well as an exegesis on Catholic tradition. This has been replicated in other forums such as the Catholic Engaged Encounter program, where many ecumenical issues come up for couples of different faiths. Often the phenomenon of anonymity works as an advantage in both actual and virtual settings on the Internet when using "The Question Box." The questions are always quite profound and sometimes rather personal. We have an e-mail version of "The Question Box" on BustedHalo.com (recently renamed "Ask Father Joe," which gives the online feature some personality) and we have received over a hundred questions on interfaith marriage issues, along with the pressing concerns of religious differences in a pluralistic world. Paulist Young Adult Ministries has added a small marriage ministry to their work and finds that the typical marriage today is an interfaith one. Most often interfaith couples do not see the differences in most religions as being a big deal, possibly because they do not practice their religions at all. However, with marriage, issues of spirituality often come along, especially with regard to family. All marriage prep programs would be wise to use a program like "The Question Box" to assist young couples in navigating through their religious differences with an eye toward pointing out moments of exclusivity as well as unity in the faith traditions. Many of the Engaged Encounter retreat weekends and pre-Cana programs in dioceses around the country already use this program, and it is often pointed out that it is the most significant moment of the experience by those in marriage prep.

Evangelical/Sacramental Catholics: Spirit and Truth/Eucharistic Adoration

I have placed these two categories together here because they are related to two contemporary young adult movements that engage both of these mindsets very well. These two groups of young adults are most often already engaged in a church community or are looking for a sense of vibrancy or a strong message from the clergy of a particular parish, religious community, or order. The Franciscan University of Steubenville, Ohio, is the major success story here, along with one of the Archdiocese of Atlanta's Young Adult Ministry programs called Spirit and Truth. Steubenville and Atlanta both use praise and worship music (better known in some circles as Christian Rock, although this has a Catholic spin to it) in liturgy and prayer services. There is always a sensual feel to the liturgy, filled with smells, bells, contemplation, and traditional religious symbols (eucharistic adoration is popular in both places). Strong preaching is often based on hard-line morality when it is offered.

With regard to the sensual experiences exhibited here, people are moved to tears and prayerful swaying, with uplifted arms as a frequent posture. To understand this group better, we need to especially look at the context of young adult life. Those that succeed in gaining evangelical young adults to their flock are often heavy-handed conservatives. However, that does not mean that the young adults themselves are conservative or even that they espouse a right-wing political mentality on issues of life. (Often these young people get co-opted into believing they are conservative because in these ritual events their religious longings are satisfied immediately by the rubrics of evangelical liturgy. Evangelical young adults are different from typical conservative Catholics because they have grown up in an age where immediate gratification is commonplace. For them, religion is like the Internet search engine Google; they expect a bolt of lightning in a religious ritual every time they attend. While they long for truth, with the expectation that an adherence to truth will fulfill their every need, they have a tough time navigating moments of ambiguity, especially death and vocational change. Mostly they rely solely on ritual experiences that utilize all their sense perceptions. They long for ritual that provides contemplation and mystery, and when ritual is based on the catechism as the central source of inspiration and guidance, they learn what is essential about the Catholic faith and they cling to these truths, professing them strongly and even occasionally excluding people who do not espouse the same devotion to tradition. Many of them can tell you *what* the church teaches but cannot tell you *why* the church teaches it. Many have no sense of the spirit of the law, but rather only a strong regard for the letter of the law. This leads to an unthinking piety that often hurts the young adult's religious sensibilities and leads them further astray from the church in the long run.

On a positive note, these young adults can bring much new life to a stagnant parish and quite often go on to be strong leaders in their parish community. I would add that the same could be said about more progressive parishes where liturgy is done well. Singable music and good relevant preaching would be hallmarks of these communities in which some sacramental/evangelical young adults find a home. They often challenge the status quo and bring a sense of adherence to Catholic tradition in parishes where it is lacking; often this is needed in many places that have relaxed into a comfortable community. Evangelical young adults have already changed the face of the church in pointing out a need for communities to espouse both the vertical and the horizontal approaches to Catholic tradition: We need to pay attention to both the mystery we know as God and to the community around us. The evangelical new faithful can help us do just that.

For Prophetic Catholics: The Jesuit Volunteer Corps

Social justice ministry continues to speak to young people. Success stories about young adults merging their faith with political action are everywhere across the Catholic spectrum. The Jesuit Volunteer Corps is just one of the many competitive service programs that exist that "ruin people for life." One young volunteer said that after she got used to living simply for a year (one of the many tenets of the organization) she could not even think of going back to her old ways of buying a CD every month. This is a group of people who both study and profess the social message of the church and live their very lives for the types of causes that they most believe in. While at times their commitment to an intentional ecclesial celebration is minimal and even their attendance at Mass sometimes wanes, these are young adults who are looking at the tenets of the Catholic faith and implementing them into their lives. The vast majority of the young adults who complete service programs are dedicated Catholics who are very active in parish and community life.

For Communal Young Adults: Theology on Tap

The ministry approach here is a social outreach that is done well in many parishes and dioceses across the country. However, the Archdioceses of Chicago and Washington distance themselves from the pack. Chicago's Father Cusick began a program nearly twenty-five years ago called Theology on Tap, which is basically a social evening coupled with a passionate speaker who talks on a given issue in the Catholic Church, on morality, issues of transition in young adult life, or an issue of secular spirituality. Some examples of speakers include Cardinal Theodore McCarrick, speaking candidly on the church's sexual abuse crisis, and a theologian debunking the popular novel *The Da Vinci Code*. "The thought was that we needed to go where [young adults] were and to treat them as adults. So we decided to serve beer in a parish setting and advertise the heck out of it. Some folks go and have the evening in a bar, but most often in Chicago we do it for four straight weeks in a parish and just serve beer there, and end the summer session with a huge picnic at the cardinal's residence," said Cusick.

Washington, DC's archdiocesan ministry rents out a local bar and is renowned for offering first-rate speakers, including Cardinal McCarrick. More important, the program has been touted by the U.S. Bishop's Conference, who often make it a priority for their young adult ministers at the diocesan level. Both programs wield symbolism well, often using the draw of their cardinal-archbishop as celebrity.

Dialogue is also often key. This is not an "I'll talk and you listen" type of thing, says one young adult. "When Cardinal McCarrick was the speaker recently he made the evening an opportunity to let young adults ask questions and make comments about what was on their mind during the sexual abuse crisis and also to respond to where the church was coming from. He listened to our experience without judgment and then offered where that experience fit in or might be enhanced by Catholic tradition as well." This is clearly the best-known program for Catholic young adults in the country.

Summary

These ministerial approaches are merely a small conglomeration of what's working well in young adult ministry. The following broad approaches are a helpful summary:

1. A ministry that is aimed intentionally at those young adults who return to the church after an absence. We need to be graciously welcoming and open to their needs and seek opportunities for interaction when they come to speak with us.
2. A need for a digital spirit in ministry. Not only is the Internet often the first place that young adults look for anything, but the instantaneous nature of the Internet is often assigned the same qualities as a religious experience. Those ministries who have a presence on the Internet not only have the distinct advantage of being most present to young adults who are anonymously searching for a spiritual message or home, but also have the advantage of providing solid informational sound bytes to feed this need for quick information.
3. A ministry that is open to dialogue. Ministries that engage in conversation are often the ones that are most effective and most popular.
4. A ministry that is rooted in mystery and Catholic tradition. Young adults long for a sense of the mysterious. They yearn for the certainty that there is something beyond themselves.
5. A ministry that is concerned for "the least among us." Social justice is no longer the church's "best kept secret." Rather, it is the essential element of Catholic tradition that even the least religiously active young adult approves of.

6. A ministry that provides life-giving community. Simply put, young adults return to parishes where they find other young adults with whom they wish to associate.

Not bad for starters. But I think we can do a whole lot better. The next part explores the young adult experience of ministry and then continues with recommendations for future ministry.

PART II
Twelve Disciples:
Two Generations

CHAPTER 3

GENERATION XERS

Community First, Contemplation Not So Much

Over the past five years, I have encountered a myriad of young adults who have been involved in ministry within the church. They often come to the church with specific longings for mystery or vibrancy in ritual. They are especially looking for a personal connection with God, some sort of experience that either lets them become more certain of their faith or at the very least gives them a connection with a tangible God. In short, they are looking for a ministry that can make God a clear entity, perhaps not exactly a ministry that helps them find a definitive answer, as Google often provides for many things they search for (if not most), but rather, one in which God becomes tangible and real for them.

The next two chapters follow twelve young adults, six from Generation X and six from the Millennial generation whom I have ministered to around the country. I offer these interviews not as a broad-ranging sociological study on young adults, but merely as an example of young adults whom I have encountered and believe do reflect a wide spectrum of the typical young adult experience within the church in both generations. Some people I interviewed have fallen away from traditional church practice, some work for the church, and others simply fit into their parish in any number of ways.

Some things to note: Obviously, this is not a representative sample of a diverse population across cultures and geographic boundaries. However, I have found some similarities that cross nearly all of the lines in this small sample that I think are worth noting. I took care to include several diverse cultures and tried to be sensitive to class and gender equity. I think that even the results here in this small sampling do speak volumes about the way that nearly all of those interviewed were ministered to in the church as young adults regarding what their spiritual longings are. It is interesting to note that the generational identity theory mentioned at the outset of the book is clearly represented by the generational differences among this group. As I pointed out at the start, several of them will probably fall within more than one type on the Bacik/Reese identifications. Let us use these interviews not merely to identify these young adults but also to examine how we minister to these types of young adults within the church. This will prove to be strong fodder for part 3.

Profile 1: Dave R., Thirty-nine, Boston, Massachusetts

Perhaps the most interesting person I spoke to was Dave. Dave has had experiences in both very conservative or traditional ministry settings and a more progressive or liberal church as well.

Dave's story begins with his straying from his Catholic tradition into a pentecostal charismatic community. He was able to find a personal connection to Christ within this community that he was unable to find within his Catholic tradition. He met a Catholic priest at one of the Christian festivals (surprisingly) who encouraged him to try to merge this experience with his Catholic roots. Dave was extremely interested in doing this because of family pressures to remain within the Catholic Church. After watching the *700 Club* (Pat Robertson's television show), he heard about a new Catholic charismatic movement at the Franciscan University at Steubenville (OH). He longed to be "on fire for Jesus" and quickly left his community college to attend the Franciscan University.

While at Steubenville, Dave felt refreshed. He went from a very rigid conservative evangelical community to the less conservative Steubenville, while maintaining some of those elements of discipline he desired and being redefined within Catholic tradition. For example, he lived in a "household" defined as a committed community of men (there were of course other "households" that were female). The prevailing attitude on campus was that the university professed "the truth" and that there was a clear sense of both Catholic identity and a personal relationship with Jesus Christ. Dave remarked to me that, in hindsight, he finds that the community at Steubenville was rather judgmental and was concerned with those who were not conservative Catholics. His roommate came into the university as an atheist and left as someone who was completely converted into a very conservative Catholic and married someone whom he met at the college.

After Steubenville, Dave joined NET (National Evangelization Teams) Ministries, a structured Catholic service organization that provides retreats for youth throughout the year, traveling around the country to do so. He paints a picture of what the lifestyle of the community was. *"It was an organization that asked for a year-long commitment to do the retreats and live in community with like six or seven other guys and then teaming up with six or seven other women to do these retreats. There was clearly an intention made to keep the men and the women separate and it was highly structured: no dating, no girls in your room, no phone calls allowed, and if I wanted to do something as simple as go and take a walk, I had to ask permission."*

Dave was a musician, playing guitar for most of the retreats, and was continually pushed to be a leader, until he started to become skeptical of their approach. He began to question the "teachings on the rules." He was no longer encouraged to be a leader after this but remained with the community, being true to his commitment to stay with the group for a year.

Dave claims, *"…the women in the group began to get a bit jaded, and this led to a lot of frustration for all of us, especially those who were feeling the same stuff, like me. We'd end up having these intense eight- or nine-hour sessions, telling one another what we felt was going wrong and who was doing what to annoy us. I just wanted to get out of there."*

Dave's problems came to a head when he began to have feelings for one of the female members of the team. *"There are no romantic relationships allowed in NET. If you have one, you're viewed as weak or no good because the rules are the rules and could even be asked to leave. If you feel like you have an attraction toward someone, you are supposed to immediately tell one of the [Franciscan] brothers."*

Instead, Dave and his "girlfriend" took their relationship underground. According to Dave, it was all rather innocent, two college kids necking out of sight of anyone else. He even admits to one session of fondling. But once they were found out, the guilt that he endured was his breaking point. *"I already felt guilty about breaking the rules, but then there was all this judgmental behavior toward me after that. I wasn't looked at the same way again. It was as if there was no possibility of redemption. I had a minibreakdown because I couldn't take it and I badly needed to get away. I mean I'm just as human as anybody else but I was made to feel like I was less than human for doing what I did. I had this revelation after I left and old friends from Steubenville heard about what I did and treated me the same way: I felt like those kids who I was trying to evangelize."*

Today, Dave lives in Boston and attends a small parish where he seems to fit in nicely. He likes his new community and points out their "commitment to social justice in real life, their contemplative stance, and the fact that they connect with who I am" is what makes the parish relevant to his experience. While it is a more liberal community, he is careful to align himself with that faction. *The bottom line for me is that I want a nonjudgmental community. I'm hypersensitive to any community that looks at things in a judgmental way. Liberals can be just as staunch in their views as conservatives! That's the downside of the liberal communities that I find at times in Boston.*

Dave firmly seeks an "adult sense of faith" and has a high regard for the teachings of Richard Rohr, a Franciscan who runs the Center for Action and Contemplation in New Mexico and who preaches *toward the middle in a very honest, down-to-earth way. His views on sexuality, justice, and a lack of judgment toward others is what I'm finding speaks to my personal spirituality these days.*

Reading Rohr has also helped him heal some of the old wounds. *He often says that most young adults start out conservative, looking at things as black or white. When black and white becomes gray there's a new need to be able to navigate in that ambiguity. I think a lot that's offered in ministry misses that point. It's been hard for me to find a community that does this well.*

Dave still longs for the same type of community feel he had at Steubenville, only with a slightly more liberal bent to it. He says that he doesn't think he could live in community anymore ("I like my personal space.") but would be happy with a community that offers an "adult sense of faith, where things aren't so straightforward. I was repeatedly told that Jesus was the answer. Jesus *was* the answer, but I wanted to know what the question was!"

Dave has hopes to become involved in Cardinal Bernardin's pet project, the *Common Ground Initiative,* where he can speak openly and without judgment to both liberals and conservatives. Dave claims that he's "still on the journey of faith" and while he's not quite sure where he's going, he's certain that he's better off than he was before.

Profile 2: Kalon G., Thirty, Los Angeles, California

Kalon G. is a rising star in the world of marketing. Brash and bright, Kalon is sought after by some of the world's biggest companies and still, as a young professional, seeks spirituality as a way to keep himself centered amidst the chaos of a hectic work life. He harkens back to his time in graduate school as a time when religion wasn't at the center of his life. As an "eclipsed" Catholic, Kalon realizes now what value religion and spirituality could have played in his life and notes his grad school years with a tinge of regret.

"My sense of purpose at that time was getting through graduate school. I was competing against some of the brightest minds in the country. It was very overwhelming, I felt like I was swimming constantly. Now I don't think church would have helped me in terms of getting through my class work but what it would've given me was perspective. I would've enjoyed my time there more and realized that it's not the end of the world if things didn't go right there. It was the first time that I was competing against a superstar every place I turned. So I think religion might have given me that sense of purpose and call to have some perspective."

The son of a traditional Catholic father and a Lutheran mother in Redondo Beach, California, Kalon also is the epitome of an ecumenical young adult. He attended a Lutheran grade school but was raised Catholic, "at least in a sacramental sense," he notes quickly. *"I'm not sure I understood the differences in religions as a child. I basically thought that catechism classes and chapel at school were complementary exercises of faith that had little difference in meaning. I had the mindset of keeping God first and really having him become an important part of my life. A lot of it had to do with praying and a lot of it had to do with my family environment."*

To support much of the latest sociological data, which claims that parents still have a strong determining factor with regard to faith, Kalon's family had a huge influence on his faith life. *"I think that my family was very supportive and I think that came through the practice of their faith. Religion, I think, gives you structure and adds meaning and discipline to your life. Especially growing up in the United States, I think. Other countries have a lot more history behind them, so I think that religion is one of the unique ties back to history that the United States lacks, being such a new country. When you look at today's times—with everyone involved in technology, dinner now lasts a mere fifteen minutes and everyone's going out to eat instead of the family being together around the dinner table—religion has become one way to tie back to your roots and it's something that you can practice every week. I think I saw that growing up. Church took my dad away from his work and my mom away from her busy life. It put us together at the dinner table saying grace every night or put us together at a service of some kind every Sunday."*

The Sunday practice of their faith as a family was rather unique in Kalon's household. *"We rotated off depending on whether it was my dad's week or my mom's week. My dad's week would be at a Catholic church near our house. My mom liked to jump around from church to church. I don't think there's really a church that she was partial to. So we'd go to the Lutheran church from my school or the Church of Religious Science, which was kind of more 'worshiping God in general.' Or we'd go to a local Bay Cities church that was kind of near the beach and got the whole God in nature experience. My mom liked to explore different avenues."*

Regardless of where the experience of Sunday worship was held, for Kalon it was simply important that rituals existed in his family. The sabbath is a concept that he holds dear, and he believes that as a country, we need more rituals, not less.

He notes, *"Ritual is, or the lack of it is, the main cause of the breakdown of the family unit. I've traveled to about twenty countries and the ones where the families are the closest are the ones that are based on ritual and the spirit of the family. Spain and Mexico are good examples. We don't have a ritual as a country really. We don't have a shared belief. We're not based on a religion or a shared belief anymore—so people end up searching for something to believe in, and everything ends up being very short-term and they end up very confused."*

This lack of shared belief and rituals connects with many young adults, who end up wandering, searching for something to believe in. Gen Xers especially note that they do not often have a solid religious or spiritual home that they call their own, and this sense of wandering often lends itself to short-term commitments instead of affiliation. Because of the variedness of young adult life, there often is not a church that holds everything young adults are looking for in one place. Gen Xers also were not often called to ritual. Often, other choices gained prominence over Sunday Mass. Soccer games, music lessons, and other family-based activities were often relegated to Sunday for children growing up. Everyone did their own thing instead of coming together with others in the neighborhood. The dismantling of the Catholic ghetto, where the parish was the center of neighborhood activities for Catholics, contributes much to the loss of communal ritual and the rise of individualism. For some ethnic immigrant communities, especially Latinos, the cultural and communal sense of coming together as a unit still exists and allows religious ritual to maintain some importance. Some lose this sense after assimilating more into American culture, but many hold on to at least some aspects of weekly ritual. While Kalon is not an immigrant, there are still signs of the importance of religious identity present in his family. Uniquely though, because he was raised in a religiously mixed family, Kalon is certainly an interesting study.

While having a particularly prayerful family that "prayed before and after every meal" and while he attended catechism classes and morning prayer in his Lutheran grade school, Kalon still found some experiences in his religious upbringing wanting: *"Going through the process of making my communion was a very strict process. We had a few very strict teachers who turned the whole thing into a responsibility as opposed to a choice— something you had to do versus something you wanted to do."*

Because of the rigid nature of his catechism program coupled with his ecumenical experiences that blurred the lines of organized religion, Kalon sought out other experiences of faith. One program in particular that Kalon remembers well was called Young Life, which he joined when he went to high school.

"It was a phenomenal program. People came from all different backgrounds—from the superstar of the school to the dropout-esque kind of person. It was nondenominational—very general. People came from all kinds of faith backgrounds. Everyone was really accepted, and I would go every week. The high school students were led by older peers—young guys in their twenties and thirties who were great mentors for the teens. I remember a guy named Don Dirks who was the head of our chapter and he was just so giving of his time. He'd plan activities for us every week, and we'd go on retreat during the summer."

Kalon reveals one of the many hallmarks of any good teen program with his experience. Mentors are sorely needed for the young, and as teens grow into young adult life they often look for similar types of mentors, people they can look up to professionally, spiritually, and personally. The rise in life coaching, psychotherapy counseling, and even personal training all point to the fact that young adults, perhaps even more than teens, want and need good mentors. Certainly, they need a different type of mentor than teens do (a point often missed by many who take on the role of young adult minister and those who employ them). Still, especially with Millennial young adults—who have such a regard for authority and often don't possess the critical tools needed for decision making and instead rely on the guidance of rules, regulations, and personal guides—the need for mentors who can help them navigate the unchartered waters of young adult ambiguities is vital.

The second vital note we can extract from Kalon's experience is the need for a community that is challenging but not judgmental. Sociologist Dean Hoge recently spoke with a group of young adult ministers at a conference in Chicago, and he cautioned all of us against judgmental attitudes in ministry outreach.

"Please, if there's one thing you can't do it's to be rigid and judgmental in your attitude toward young adults. That's one thing that certainly won't work for the large majority of those outside the church. You're not going to gain converts like that. You need to have a strong sense of welcome for this group, give them a sense that they are wanted and loved. They can withstand a good challenge, but you can't go overboard."[1]

Kalon's college experiences with faith-based communities epitomize Hoge's example perfectly: *"In college, I became active with a few other religious organizations, and the thing that really bothered me was that they were really focused on the act of sinning and that the people involved were all sinners. It was all*

'How can we be so privileged that God would spend any time with us at all? Because we're all bad people and sin on a daily basis we need to always ask God for forgiveness, over and over.' Now I think that could be good and I think there's a good reflective aspect to that style and being aware of our sins and shortcomings, but I think there was too much focus on this and it became too negative. I think that inherently people are good, and I think there are aspects of the world that can [make them] stray from being good. So I don't like to focus on the negative aspects as much. Needless to say, I didn't find a whole lot of what I was looking for here. The strange thing is that the people that I remember as being very gung-ho for this kind of program ended up straying from religion altogether down the road."

Kalon was looking for a welcoming community, and church organizations left him empty in this regard. However, the fraternity system at his local college became a great surrogate church.

"What actually became a churchlike experience for me was my fraternity. Sigma Chi was founded on Christian beliefs, and our symbol is the white cross. Even in our fraternity ritual, we have to accept that God exists. This was very tough for a lot of guys. There was a lot in that ritual that was based on religious belief. The fundamentals are seen in the closeness of the group. In college outside of this fraternity situation I found I had more of an individual spirituality because I didn't really have a church or an organized group that I was a part of. But in the fraternity, they believed that when you have a group of people together who were performing a ritual or convening together that there is something more powerful than them that exists. It was the whole 'When two or three are gathered in my name' kind of thing."

Interestingly enough, church community was easily replaced by an organization that had indeed a strong sense of welcome and challenge: a brotherhood, if you will. Kalon felt like part of an extended family in Sigma Chi, and his belief in God grew stronger in a communal sense (where he found belief in at least a higher power of some kind to be present) in the life he shared with his friends. Naturally, their philanthropic sense as a fraternal organization solidified this sense even more. The sad truth of the matter is that when church community fails it is all too easily replaced, at least in the short term. There are many choices that can easily be cheap substitutes for the richness that religious faith can offer, and yet these substitutes on a whole also feed young adults well for at least a short period of time.

Kalon notes, *"A huge advantage for the Catholic Church is that it has been around and strong for thousands of years. The importance of going through the ritual of the Mass, which has a lot of meaning and structure to it, is central here. Having a track record or a tradition to back you up makes the faith credible because despite the variety of beliefs in the church, nobody ever really strays too far from the basic tenets. When you look at some of the newer churches, you can't be sure what it is that they are based on, or even what they really believe. Some of them are simply trying too hard to be modern instead of providing a balance."*

So while Kalon's fraternity experience gave him an overwhelming sense of brotherhood and the importance of tradition, he didn't necessarily gravitate toward the Catholic Church for the same reasons. Why? Simply put, the judgmental community was enough to send him elsewhere to seek a place with a traditional mindset, good rituals, and philanthropic opportunities to give back to others.

As he left college, Kalon spent a good deal of time in Los Angeles, where he was not really involved in a church; working and attending graduate school was taking precedence. Yet Kalon notes that it wasn't for a lack of trying to be involved in a church community.

"I didn't find much for young professionals in LA in terms of church experience. LA's a tough city because it's very spread

out. In a city like New York it's easy to jump on the subway and get around anywhere in about fifteen minutes, so it's easy to find a group that you're looking for. It's a lot more difficult in LA to simply find things. I was also traveling quite a bit for work then, and when I was in graduate school it simply came down to a time commitment. Looking back on it, I wish church had been a greater part of my life, because I think that was a time when I really needed it."

The importance of being visible in the outside community for young adults will become a future hallmark for young adult ministry. Kalon notes that *"access is key. People don't know where to look. The Journey Church [which he talks about later in this interview] did one thing well—they marketed themselves very successfully. They printed their worship services on the back of a subway map and gave it away with a metro card [a subway fare card for the NYC transit system]. On blazing hot days they gave away free water bottles with attached cards listing the times for the Journey services. It sat on my desk for five or six weeks, and finally I said that I was going to check it out."*

With not only other churches, but other activities competing for their attention more than ever before, churches need to market themselves creatively without becoming overly superficial. Kalon talked to me about the good and the bad in marketing church.

"I joined the Journey Church when I moved to New York after grad school—another nondenominational group and I led a 'growth group'—a weekly reading group. It would be about ten or fifteen people gathered in a very casual "come as you are" atmosphere. Their tagline was, "a casual contemporary Christian church." So I went there for awhile but I couldn't get past the lack of sacred space I felt in this group. Something important for a church is location and the feeling that is projected when you are in a group—that whole sense of sacred space. The Journey started in the Promenade Theater on the West Side of Manhattan,

and it had a very familial feel to it. But their primary goal was to grow. It was clearly stated in every meeting. They announced how many new members they had and how many groups we had meeting. Everything was listed every single week, and I think in all of that—the message got lost. And when they moved to a larger theater they held the meetings in a huge auditorium with no personality. There was no warmth to it—no familial feeling to it. The message was still bring your friends out and give big— how much money are you giving to the church? They pushed tithing a lot. It was kind of an extreme attempt to garner financial support. Then they tried to tie their weekly message back to movies or more contemporary pop culture things, and it became a very shallow message. I never felt like I gained any insight or got something out of my time spent there. In fact I walked away feeling quite empty actually, which was surprising because when I first joined and it was much smaller, I walked away feeling really good. In big cities like New York or LA you're really looking for that kind of connection, and when you find it, it's quite exciting. But eventually those feelings left, and I ended up leaving. It felt like a big marketing ploy or pyramid scheme."

What has Kalon found in his recent spiritual experience that captured a sense of his longings? And what was it that brought him to that experience? He was recently reintroduced to the Catholic Church by his girlfriend.

"I'm always willing to try a new experience, and I ended up going to a few churches with her on Sundays. She also invited me on a retreat [my ministry's BustedHalo retreat program, where I met Kalon]. I would have to say the retreat was easily the best I've had of all of my religious experiences with any groups or gatherings. I think it renewed my belief, and also with a lot of the bad press that the Catholic Church has gotten lately, I think the retreat really showed me where the power in the faith lies. And I think that power lies between the balance of the tradition and the balance of the questioning of the tradition and *making sure that the tradition is still applicable today. And that's what I found valuable in the retreat."*

One of the hallmarks of the retreat program is a respect for spiritual questions. This retreat in particular had a lively group of people gathered together to explore their own questions and struggles of faith individually in silent reflection and then again in both large and small group conversations. They would glean insights from a presentation given by another young adult and were encouraged to ask questions in an open forum later in the weekend. The wisdom of the Catholic tradition was always highlighted by the staff but with a respect for the wisdom of individual experience as well. This helped forge not only an atmosphere of safe space, where people felt free and open to express their own struggles without fear of reprisal or of being judged, but also a strong sense of community where people reached out to one another at their deepest place of woundedness in many ways.

Kalon notes, *"It was amazing that we had people there from very diverse careers, who were so talented and offering so much of themselves. Nobody knew one another, but by the end of the weekend such a special bond was created. It was totally like my fraternity experience and the whole 'where two or three are gathered in my name I am present' thing. Meeting good people who allow you to grow is key. So many people just sap your energy and take so much from you. But when you go on a retreat people there are putting their faith ahead of getting their hair done or trying the newest restaurant or the trendy night-club. Their focus is on more than themselves. So it's good that I'm searching for that."*

Finally, a sense of mystery and tradition captures Kalon every time he returns to a Catholic church. *"I also find that in the Catholic Church the churches themselves are interesting. I find them very comforting especially when I'm in a big city. Because you can go in and suddenly you are back in Italy years ago. You can go to any country and walk into a church and get the same kind of feeling because it's the same kind of environment and the same ritual. It's a wonderful unifying feeling."*

One of the biggest turnouts for events that I have seen with young adults are church tours. At St. Paul the Apostle Parish we have had young adults research and lead a tour of the Paulist Church in Midtown Manhattan, and people have come out for it over and over. One of the Paulists now leads a tour during the Christmas season as a result of that success.

Right now Kalon has no church community since returning to LA, but he feels his faith life is strong and prays a lot with his girlfriend, Maria, who lives only a short plane ride away in San Francisco. Both now have new jobs on the West Coast, after spending time in New York, where they first met.

"I want something that's quality and not quantity. I need a place where I feel nourished. The homily, to me, is the most important part of a Sunday service. What a pastor has to say is very important to me. Some of the churches I've been to have had homilies that are so shallow or so meaningless. One compared Spiderman to faith, another talked about the Terminator. I would come away thinking that this is just one big marketing tool that's just as shallow as the movie Spiderman is itself. It's fun to watch, but did I really learn anything from it? Not really. So I'm looking for something with meaning that has that intimacy or closeness that I found on the retreat. And someplace where I can do something philanthropic—giving back in many ways is church in itself. I don't need that every Sunday, but when I get it once in awhile it has rich meaning for me because when you get people who want to be at a church service as opposed to people who are there out of obligation, you'll get people who'll risk more. They won't just sit there and try not to fall asleep, but they'll really be getting something out of being there. That kind of atmosphere also needs to be reflected by the clergy and the staff as well. It needs to be a place where everybody's excited to go there."

Kalon also notes that a huge mistake that some churches make is that *"sometimes some church groups try to dumb things down a bit. I mean one group who tried to attract college students from schools like NYU and Columbia in New York was trying to attract them with a dumbed-down message! Come on! These are two of the top schools in the nation and you're trying to dumb it down! It doesn't make a whole lot of sense. The message needs to be intellectual, articulate, and it has got to tie in global issues, world problems, and modern-day society. It's got to take the wisdom of the past and apply that to the present day— what is going on in our lives as we exist."*

His final note suggests that *"being active in the community and providing outreach to the community you are in is also important, and tying that in to the weekly ritual experience in some way—even if that pushes the envelope a bit in terms of the usual practice of ritual—is crucial. But again, it needs to be balanced with the tradition itself. Why are we doing this? Because our faith has taught us that this is important. Putting that together would be a great experience for me and I hope to find that soon."*

Profile 3: Rachel B., PhD, Thirty-five, Theologian, New York City (By Way of Jacksonville, Albany, and Boston)

Raised in a Filipino Catholic household in middle of a Protestant culture, where it was hard to understand who you are as a Catholic, Rachel attended Catholic school for her entire life up until college. She did not really notice how Catholic she was until she got to college when suddenly *"a holy day of obligation would roll around and I didn't have someone right there who was going to march me off to the church right next door anymore.*

So I asked myself 'Do I go? Do I not go? Does it mean anything to me if I don't go?' Second, and I think this is a common experience in college, you've got people from other religious traditions around, and people are just comparing notes or even experimenting with not practicing or not being religious for the first time because now they actually have a choice about it."

Rachel herself dabbled in a few different religious expressions while always being true to her Catholic self. *"I was involved in the Catholic campus ministry for sure, but I was also involved in singing in a gospel choir. So I engaged myself in a Protestant conversation as well as a Catholic one. We had a fairly divided campus ministry between traditional folks who liked smells and bells, progressive folk, and Opus Dei. So I was also muddling through those different boxes and trying to figure out 'What kind of Catholic am I?' It took me most of college to even figure that question out, and by the time I did it was time to go!"*

This experience of defining her Catholicism and being engaged in conversation with other religious traditions colored her way of valuing liturgy. She longed to find a community that she could appreciate as much as she did in college and could not find one in her hometown of Jacksonville. When asked about specifics she would be looking for in a parish, Rachel does not hesitate in responding. *"One of the things I loved about campus ministry was that there was space for questioning. And I didn't find that same space in these other places. I found out in college that there were many ways of being Catholic. You might be more or less a devotional person or a social justice or community activist person, but those are all very precious and valuable ways of being engaged with your faith. I liked that there was space in campus ministry to hold all these different pieces of religious identity together."*

Rachel's faith radically shifted in college. She had been focused on devotions in her Filipino Catholic household, *"and that really didn't work for me. My mom is very into Virgin Mary stuff, the bleeding hearts sort of scenario. We had wall-to-wall icons in our house, lots of rosaries, and lots of candles. If you didn't know you were in a house because of the stacks of laundry or the smell of food in the kitchen, you'd think you were in a shrine!"*

She finally told her parents that she would go to church on her own because she could not stand the parish that they regularly attended. *"Honestly, that meant I wasn't going at all. I really looked too! I figured maybe if I don't find it in the church that I grew up in, maybe somebody else has it. But I wasn't successful at that, and I finally gave up. So instead of going to church, I would actually go to the beach and just yell at God! This actually lasted for about two years! I thought I was getting more out of that than trying to wedge myself into a community that wasn't sure if they even wanted to have me."*

Clearly a sense of welcome in her parents' parish and even in the other parishes in the area was lacking. Rachel was like many others who often find themselves in a parish that allows them to be anonymous, doesn't respect or invite their gifts and talents, and maintains the same leaders in liturgy and ministry without refueling these approaches with new blood.

Once Rachel left her parents' home for Upstate New York, she immediately made plans to look for a community again. It's important to note, as previously mentioned, that here we have someone who was not engaged in traditional religious practice for over two years but it is obvious that spiritual longings were still present in her. She looked to find a community away from the small farming village she lived in *"because I wanted to open my world up a little bit. So I would drive fifty miles to the closest city and try to find a parish there. I was actually on my way to a mall on the outskirts of town when I saw a sign for Saturday 5 p.m. Mass, and I thought I'd head in. I'm sure we've all had the experience where we've been so touched by a sermon that you feel like the priest is talking directly to you. I couldn't tell you now what he said but I had the feeling at the time that I was being profoundly addressed. I also remember weeping, not sad weeping, but like…I'm home weeping. I started singing in my pew, and then I returned the next week and sang again, and the choir director came up to me and asked me if I'd like to be the cantor. My response was, 'But you don't even know me!' And he said, 'Well I know you can sing and that's enough for me!' So just from that invitation I became involved in the life of the community. I suppose if I had been singing badly he wouldn't have said anything, but the fact that he identified my gifts and was aware of them was great."*

Here are three words that you will need to learn and remember: DIRECT…PERSONAL… INVITATION. There is no other way to make sure that young adults are included and active in the life of your parish or ministry. Young adults can easily be anonymous in your community if you let them, but they long to be invited and often do not have the moxie to invite themselves into parish life. They are often strangers in a strange land, especially because of the overwhelming lack of other people like them in parishes. Many are fearful of being the only young person in a parish and, especially Gen Xers, hope to be engaged in community with other people their age. Their spirituality is inherently tied to seeing themselves engaged with other people. At the same time, Rachel points out that *"[this parish] didn't really have a 'young adult anything' but it just happened to be a welcoming place with good preaching."* Those hallmarks make all the difference for both Gen X and Millennial young adults.

Rachel began to feel the call to ministry at this juncture of her life. *"But I knew it wasn't to be a nun,"* she remarks. *"Well, if I'm being called to priesthood, what do I do with that?"* She applied to Harvard Divinity School soon after to immerse herself in study and to discern where a possible call to ministry might indeed lie. *"I knew I wasn't going to change religions or anything, so I just decided not to think about priesthood but thought I would just keep working in education and social work school.*

Harvard doesn't have a social work school; the closest thing they had was the divinity school. But I found out that the two are really nothing alike! I decided to sort it out when I got there, and I got placed in a really fabulous place for my field work. They had a woman pastoral associate there and other women on staff in leadership positions, so it wasn't just priests."

Rachel's job consisted of being "on call" at the parish's front desk and greeting people off the street who would come in for various reasons. *"Sometimes people would want something simple like a Mass card, but other times people would come in and say 'I'm homeless. I have nothing to eat. How can you help me?' Or people would actually come in with a traumatic spiritual crisis, and then what do you do with that? So it was interesting to get this opportunity to have to think on your feet, spiritually. This was pretty hard for an introvert, so I just had to keep doing it!"*

Rachel also did certain projects with the religious education director, but the thing she treasured most was being trained as a lay preacher and presider. *"I had some training already in my coursework [Rachel also took courses at the renowned Weston School of Theology, run by the Jesuits], but my parish community was intentional about selecting people for formation in this capacity.*

"I remember early on almost being paralyzed by the thought that there were people out there according me some kind of moral authority to talk with them. It's really humbling." Her prayer life continued to deepen so well that she likened it to "being in water." When you're in water it surrounds you; it's always there. Rachel notes, *"[Prayer] was something that was happening all the time whether I was actively engaged in it or not. I needed to realize that even being actively engaged with another person might also be prayer."*

Rachel's experience of being in Boston has made her quite demanding of what she expects church to be. She is a tough audience and a ruthless critic of bad liturgy because she sees how wonderful it is when things are done well and a community is engaged with one another and with Christ at the center of it all. Likewise, she believes that there is no excuse for a community not to be engaging and is eager to vote with her feet when it is not. Her experience is typical of young adults one does not see week in and week out in the pews. The same old boring and staid homily is not worth the young adult's time (or anyone else's really!). A community that simply goes through the motions of liturgy is one in which a young adult, be they Millennial or Gen X, is not willing to be part of. Frankly, we can learn a lot from young adults about the importance of ritual. Do we tell the stories well? Do we engage people with preaching? Do we let them know they are wanted and appreciated? Is ritual simply a great place to kill an hour, or is it something we value? Rachel hopes that setting the bar high doesn't disappoint her too much.

To date she has not found a community in her new home in New York that is as engaging as her old community in Boston. *"I haven't found a Catholic place that measures up. People are surprised that liturgy in New York is a lot more restrictive, especially when it comes to women's leadership."* When asked if she feels welcome as a woman in the Catholic Church in New York, Rachel offers a surprising answer: *"As a straight woman, I have to say that I think I'd be more welcome if I were a gay or lesbian person. I say that because, and I could be wrong, but there is so much more attention paid to that kind of difference that the woman part gets less care or attention from folks. It's like you have secular woman and church woman, and secular woman has a lot more latitude with how she can be. Church woman is a lot more circumscribed, I find. You're expected to act a certain way, and when you don't…what're they going to do, ignore me?"*

Rachel describes her religiosity today as "patchwork." She is a theologian by day at Union Theological Seminary, where she completed her doctoral degree and also serves as a music minister in a variety of churches of various denominations. *"There are some Sundays where I've just maxed out on God! I think God understands when I need a break. I serve in an Episcopal chaplaincy where the priest is a woman, and I appreciate the way she does church, but I also serve at a Catholic parish with a Jesuit, and I really appreciate the way he does church. So I'm stitching together these pieces to approximate some semblance of a spiritual home. It's imperfect, and I get rained on every once in awhile but there it is. Not the best situation, but it's livable. I wouldn't want to do this forever."*

As a theologically educated woman, Rachel has been invited by many colleagues who have left the Catholic Church to be ordained in other denominations. They ask why she bothers to stay *"in a church that doesn't make space for [her]. And that's something that I have to deal with every day. People have told me that if I come over [to their denomination], 'we will fast-track you to ordination.' But I am very clear to them when I say that there is no sense in my leaving until my leaving feels more like a gain than a loss. After all, it's not that community that is calling me. I mean I'm happy to work with those traditions and be a music minister for them, but it always feels like going over as a guest worker. They will never be MY community. I feel called to my tradition, not another one."*

Rachel reports that her personal prayer life is in a "fuzzy space right now." There is a huge temptation to be lazy about prayer because *"I'm doing this all the time; I mean, when am I not praying? When it's going well, it's like being in a band, and you have been playing together so long that you can read one another's rhythms and faces and everything. And all I have to do is look up and we all know exactly what to do—that kind of seamless communication."*

I often wonder myself why Rachel remains in the Catholic Church, and yet I know that the church is indeed enriched by people like her. She has the gifts and talents that would be great in a role like the diaconate, a role that, based on church history, many believe may open to women in the future in both the Orthodox and Catholic traditions. Many believe that there is a historical precedent in place to make this viable. However, only time will tell. Like other Gen Xers her age, Rachel's spirituality is less individualistic when you separate what she discerns as a vocational call out of the mix. It is connected with community and her place in it. She does not prefer the sheer solitude that many Millennials enjoy, but ironically, when community is lacking in a particular church, Rachel wastes no time in heading to the beach. Her God listens to her venting, whether it involves an inability to find a welcoming community or a frustration with a church that tells her she is not called to ordination when she clearly feels a call to ministry and often feels second-best as a lay minister. Regardless, she has stayed in the church this long, and her gift to the people of God in all their various denominations to whom Rachel offers service might simply be to do just that.

Profile 4: Gregory P., Thirty-seven, Psychotherapist, Marriage Minister, Steubenville, Ohio

Greg was raised in the Charismatic Renewal and went through the Life in the Spirit program when he was eight, *"whereupon [he] received 'Baptism in the Spirit' and the 'gift of tongues.' Following this, [he] had a personal and deep encounter of the Holy Spirit in each sacrament [he] received from first confession through matrimony."*

Greg never left the church, though he *"spent significantly more time with evangelical Protestants than Catholics, and has had periods when [he] seriously questioned [his] faith and [has] been seriously questioned [sometimes virulently] about [his] faith."*

Greg has been around many different forms of ministry in his work with both the Franciscan University at Steubenville, where he serves occasionally as adjunct faculty, and in his radio ministry for Ave Maria Radio. While I often disagree with his points of view, I have a profound respect for his experiences with faith communities and his objectivity in describing those communities.

Greg describes his experience with progressive/liberal ministries as ones that *"focus primarily on relationship building with varying degrees of success. At best, they provide a sense of community from which to build a greater sense of personal faith. At worst, it is a case of the blind leading the blind, which substitutes relationship and affirmation for serious conversion and faith formation."* As Greg previously described in his stages of faith theory, he thinks that liberal communities often *"work best for those who are in the sensualist/spiritual stage of religious devotion—people who need a community to believe in but have not yet matured to the point of developing an understanding of the ideology that unites that community. These groups can be very helpful, especially for those who have been turned off by religious people in the past, but they can be problematic if they exalt relationships within the group (or personal affirmation) as an end in itself."*

Greg is also cautious of typically conservative ministry groups. In his opinion, *"It is important not to paint these groups with too wide a brush. I know several very healthy, spiritually mature people who participate in such organizations; these groups can, for the spiritually immature, be very dangerous."* He also believes that if a person has some spiritual maturity, groups like Opus Dei or the Legionnaires of Christ offer some wonderful tools for helping the laity actualize their common priesthood—empowering them to consecrate the world (and especially the world of work) to Christ. Greg adds, *"I do agree, though, that there are dangers for those who don't have the psychological or spiritual maturity to weigh advice they are given in direction with their own good sense: treating the comment of a spiritual director as gospel. When they do not work well, these groups can be a breeding ground for rigorism and psychopathology."*

Greg is most comfortable with what he calls "dynamic orthodoxy." The importance of an intimate personal relationship to both God and others is encouraged, as is the need to develop a healthy understanding/personal integration of a traditional faith capable of responding to contemporary needs. Dynamic orthodoxy is constantly being challenged to prove itself distinct from mere conservatism (with which it is often confused) and to defend itself against attacks from both the right and the left. For example, the Franciscan University at Steubenville is regularly criticized in Catholic conservative newspapers like *The Wanderer* for its charismatic worship and emotive spirituality and is also regularly vilified by the *National Catholic Reporter* as "a bastion of retrograde conservatism." As an example from Greg's own ministry, *"Promoting Natural Family Planning is an important part of my ministry to couples and families, so I am loathed by conservatives for promoting 'a contraceptive mentality' and laughed at by liberals for being 'hopelessly out of touch with the mainstream.'"*

Greg makes a good point here. In our own personal relationship, we have disagreements about issues because I often find him overly conservative. Meanwhile, his conservative friends call him a liberal. Greg does not claim allegiance with either side, choosing to align himself with a new breed of faith tradition. While I find his theology, and Steubenville's, ideologically conservative, I think they have also contributed something well worth looking at for young adult ministry, and that is the need for emotive faith experiences that are more than mere sensual experiences. We can no longer allow our ministries and churches to continue to provide young adults with the same old staid and boring experiences that they have been exposed to over recent years. Experiences on college campuses suggest that young adults are certainly looking to merge the secular with the sacred. Tom Beaudoin also suggests that young adults are settling for the religious experiences that they find lurking in pop culture rather than to accept what the church presents as ritual experience. While I do not think that the rigidness of Greg's orthodoxy is the answer to the young adult problem, I do think that he does have much that is positive in his approach, and his contribution will assist in the next wave of ministry with those in their twenties and thirties. At the very least I think Greg's version of orthodoxy is somewhat of a better and more toned-down version than what is frequently offered. Greg at least wants to have a conversation with those of an immature faith and attempts to move them to a more adult faith. I fear that many of the groups that Colleen Carroll describes are in favor of placing those who disagree with them to the outside and then leaving the outcasts to fend for themselves spiritually. Greg might also agree with this mentality but only after trying to engage the dissenters in the tradition and only then, if there continues to be disagreements with the tenets of the faith, will people be asked to leave. At the very least, I have to give Greg credit for trying to reach out to young people, even if the end result is the same. Greg's experience as a faith-filled person has given him the opportunity to place that experience in the context of an evangelical ministry. His is a ministry that offers promise but still leaves me cautiously hesitant. Regardless, his experience as an evangelical young adult is one that reveals much to us about the contribution that evangelicals have to make to the church.

While both Colleen Carroll and Greg suggest that young adults are returning to orthodox traditions, these traditions are significantly different from what those in a more progressive camp may fear to be psychologically unhealthy. The problem that the reclaiming of older traditions presents is an internal problem in church politics, with rigorous conservatives taking advantage of the spiritually illiterate and progressive traditions not providing these old traditions in new and unusual forms. Polarization occurs within the church in which a progressive camp is seen as choosing to combat the conservative pole of the church in a game of "liturgical stratego," where fear breeds contempt on both sides.

Profile 5: Dan T., Thirty-seven, Brooklyn, New York

Dan's experience is an interesting one: *"In my early years the church was something I had to do because it was expected—we were Catholic after all; it's what we did. No explanation, no questioning. When it came time for me to be an altar boy, of course I would do it—it's what was expected. In eighth grade I received a full scholarship to attend Cathedral Preparatory Seminary in Brooklyn. The amazing thing was I had not applied to Cathedral— they had sought me out. Why? I was a senior altar boy, and in my parish it was generally felt among some, including several priests, that I was a strong candidate for the priesthood. One day before Mass I was talking with the youngest priest in our parish about what high school I should choose. Father Bob told me that I should not go to Cathedral Prep precisely because that was what everyone else expected. He asked what I wanted to do, if I wanted to be a priest. I started to say 'Well,' and he stopped me and said, 'If you have to say that, then you shouldn't be a priest. Find your own path in life.' He was the first priest that in my eyes saw who I was and not who I was expected to be."*

Dan entered high school instead at the renowned Jesuit school, Regis, in New York City, where he had his next positive experience with the clergy.

"In my freshman theology class, Father Stephen Duffy was the teacher. He immediately started the class off by saying, 'I don't care if you know the precepts of the church. I don't want to know if you go to church on Sunday and whether you believe in God or not; that's your own business. That is all for a religion class. This is a theology class, and we are here to discuss morality.' He simply blew me away. Father Duffy that year introduced us to opening our minds to challenging our church, to accept some of the ideas of other religions or at least to test them. He let me know that I could be closer to God without having to be close to the church."

Dan was a fairly typical Catholic who went to Mass on occasion, but it was never a mandate for him as it was in the days of his childhood. What ended up driving him away from the church, possibly for good, was planning for his wedding. Dan's fiancée, Sheila, went through a parish RCIA program and converted to Catholicism, thinking it would make things that much easier with their wedding plans. After her conversion, the couple found out that they would not be able to have their ceremony outdoors as they had planned, but that it would have to be in a church building. Ironically, instead of Sheila remaining Lutheran, her conversion created further difficulties. *"So trying to get closer to the Roman Catholic Church actually caused us more problems and drove us further away. The combination of the regulations that the church imposed coupled with how spiritual and moving our wedding ceremony actually turned out to be made me really wonder why I belonged to a church that seemed out of touch with what was important, namely that God is everywhere, not just in specific buildings so designated. And that the most important thing Jesus told us was to love one another—it's as simple as that. At this point I don't know if I could become active in a church community anymore, because promoting or supporting a church I had problems with would be hypocritical. I believe that spirituality and community can be achieved outside the parameters of a church."*

Dan has clearly become an ecumenical young adult who has little patience for the differences among the religious sects of Christianity. He is not concerned about church regulations or ecclesiology, but has more of a simple faith—loving people whom he comes into contact with no matter what happens and in general living a very upstanding moral life.

As far as belief in a personal God, Dan does not believe God is acting directly in the lives of people, but is more subtle. *"I don't believe that God cares if we follow all the rules set down by whatever religion we belong to—to me that characterizes God as a micromanaging, egotistical being—and I cannot believe that she or he is like that. With that being said, I still see a divine influence all the time all around me—mostly within people or in people's actions, particularly when they're not motivated by religious authority but rather by their own accord. I can see God in nature, in the seemingly random nature of the universe, which scientists keep discovering has some order. I see a 'divine architecture' in the world and in humanity—where individual actions do have influences they may not foresee simply because we are all part of the same creation. Where do these beliefs come from? I can't say that they come from any one specific source. I do believe that my Regis/Jesuit education played a huge role in my thought process simply because it encouraged me to question things and find out what my own beliefs were. I'll relate another story about Father Duffy—he told us once of an alum who came to him with the news that he was getting married, but the girl was Jewish and he was converting to Judaism. Father Duffy asked him one question—was he doing it for her or for himself. The guy answered he was doing it for himself, to* which Father Duffy replied, 'Then you are closer to God then you were before.'"

For Dan, the inconsistency of the church runs deep, and that is a personal barrier to being a member for him. *"I left two Irish cultural organizations because of the church. Both started adding "born and unborn" at the end of the Pledge of Allegiance, and part of our dues started going to the Right to Life Party. When I questioned this I was told, 'We are Catholics; we have to do this.' It really hurt to walk away. I have not been a part of an Irish community like them since, and it's something I miss dearly. As to whether I agree with most if the church's tenets—I'm not sure. I think in many ways the true meaning of what it means to be Christian has been lost because of the hierarchy, politics, and 'tenets' set down by Rome. But being a Christian should mean that all you need is love—the most important thing Jesus ever said was, 'Love one another as I have loved you.' Yes, this is a central part of church teaching, but why can't women teach it? Why can we only celebrate a marriage in a designated building? What it comes down to is that I believe in the core ideal of the church, but not the structure that has formed around it."*

Dan is an interesting case because he has clearly had some good experiences with the church—some of them even seem to have formed him in profound ways spiritually—but it wasn't enough to keep him around. I asked him if there was still something positive lurking in the church for him.

"I do recognize that there are positive things within the church. For all the things I disagreed with him on, John Paul II was a very good man. There are plenty of good people in the church, and as I said before, the core belief is one I am entirely behind. But then, I can say the same about the core belief in many other Christian denominations as well. I would also say that it wasn't only the bad experiences that pushed me away, but the good experiences, those that made me question things, motivated me as well. I've said it before, that if the Jesuits ever

*decided to split from the church, I'd be first in line at their church.
It was the Jesuit teachings—at both Regis and the University of
Detroit—that started me on this path."*

Here we have an interesting crossroads. The Jesuits, who
challenged Dan to think for himself and formed his spirituality
in obviously very profound and adult ways, also were not able to
give him an experience of the church that was enough for him
to value the inherent culture of Catholicism. At the same time,
perhaps the logistical concerns around his marriage could have
been resolved in a compromise from the church's standpoint.
Clearly Cusick's theory on the "moments of return" is certainly
proven with Dan's example. Regardless, perhaps Dan needed
more pastoral care than the church (or at least his church) was
willing to provide. Dan did get married in the church after his
outdoor wedding at the Regis High School chapel. He continues
to hold the Jesuits in high regard, but his practice of his faith is
minimal at best.

Profile 6: John C., Thirty, Westchester County, New York

John grew up in Jamaica, Queens, a section of the most
diverse borough of New York City. His parish experience growing up was quite an interesting one: a traditional parish with mul-
tiethnic sensibilities. John speaks of the celebration of liturgy
being rather traditional there, but there was also a constant infu-
sion of elements of African-American, Portuguese, or Latin
American culture into the liturgy and into the life of the parish.
He was heavily involved in the parish as an altar server, lector,
member of the St. Vincent de Paul society, and director of a summer program for children. He enjoyed both a sacramental life in
his community as well as the opportunities he had for service.

From this experience, John went to Cathedral Prep High School, where he found the environment *"much stricter and by the book."* John mentioned that he liked their *"toned-down version of Mass because [he had] a hard time concentrating when there's too much singing."* Yet he still felt that something in his liturgical experience was lacking compared to his memories of his home parish, where he felt more comfortable.

Fordham University gave John his first nontraditional look at liturgy. While he felt that it *"wasn't particularly traditional,"* he felt that sometimes liturgy was a good experience nonetheless. John stated that his problem with changing the way liturgy was done was simply that *"sometimes it was change for change's sake. For example, oftentimes the university's campus ministry staff would announce that 'during the eucharistic prayer the tradition here is to stand.' While I don't have a problem with someone standing during the consecration, if I feel that this is the most important part of the Mass and feel more reverent kneeling, I don't want to feel pressured to stand either. It was never properly explained why they wanted us to stand either. It was just kind of judgmental in my eyes."*

John was part of the Right to Life Club, which had no connection to the campus ministry. John mentions that they were more than merely a vocal protest group on campus about abortion; they also *"visited a women's shelter and a home for abandoned children and provided some service to them."* I asked if they concerned themselves with issues like capital punishment as well and John, a lawyer, noted that *"we didn't really cover that, but while it's a very different issue from abortion, most of the people in the pro-life club were probably against capital punishment. It's kind of a shame that we didn't do much on this because now I know as a lawyer that we probably could've had a good deal of influence legislatively because capital punishment laws vary from state to state."*

While in law school at Fordham John became very disconnected from the church mostly because of the time constraints of his studies. *"I got into a lot of bad spiritual habits, and it was hard to get back into doing things again. You just feel that you have no time for anything, and while prayer and church often helps with that, there was that discipline that I was lacking."*

John has since returned to the parish of his youth in Jamaica, even though he has moved to Westchester County. He said that he *"looked for what I came from and didn't find it."* So he simply returned to the parish he felt most at home in.

The most appealing aspect of John's home parish is the fact that the community is *"small, connected, and homey while being traditional and yet culturally diverse. I tried a parish in Manhattan known for its young adult ministry programming, but it just felt way too big to me. I really liked the smaller, more intimate community."*

John prefers a traditional liturgy because of its *"constant feel. There's always a struggle between changing and not changing. I guess I'm more comfortable with slow change in the church. When change is too quick, I'm tempted to ask if we were right all along."*

For now, John still has some longings in parish life. He wishes that his parish offered *"constant community service programs. I miss coaching in the youth baseball league. Those service experiences led me to a deeper inner prayer life."*

John concluded the interview by saying that he doesn't think his experiences at Fordham have made him *"less traditional. But I do think I've become more relaxed about certain things. Studying a lot of theology and philosophy has taught me a lot about doubt, and going through that, it's been hard to quantify my self-reflecting experience, but I know it's a lot more than knowing stuff."*

CHAPTER 4

MILLENNIAL YOUNG ADULTS

Rules Rule! Moments of Peace and Living for Today

Profile 1: Candice R., Twenty-two, Medical Student, Chicago Suburbs

As a prospective doctor, Candice R. understands a patient's holistic needs. She recently mentioned the deep effect that September 11th had on her college community during her freshman year at the University of Illinois, where she was a semiactive member of the Catholic Newman Center.

"I had gone to Catholic school nearly all my life, and now here I was as part of this state institution when I realized in the midst of this tragedy that not everyone here is even Christian. I had some fascinating discussions with people on my floor in the dorm who were Hindu, Buddhist, and other denominations. I started to wonder in my premed mindset about how different religions might affect a doctor-patient relationship. So I really wanted to learn about different religions, and I subsequently became a religious studies major. I wanted to be able to stand my ground, to know my Catholic faith and be able to stand up for it, but also respect other people for their religious convictions and try to understand where they are coming from. As a physician it's better to understand the whole patient and not just their physical ailments."

As the child of Filipino immigrants, Candice grew up religious. *"I think it has to do with the Filipino culture. I just remember the church always being a significant part of our lives. Even when my parents first came here from the Philippines they weren't really established, and although we didn't have much to our name, using food stamps and everything, they still made time to go to church and even more, to volunteer at church. So I always thought that was really interesting."*

As the Catholic ghetto has disintegrated with the rise of a highly transient culture, young adults often do not have a place to call their spiritual home. One of the exceptions to this phenomenon is young adults who belong to families with a strong ethnic identity, like Latinos and Filipinos. Most young adults in North America today have not been brought up in the ethnically rooted Catholic cultures of their parents and grandparents, with ethnic parishes that defined neighborhood boundaries and secluded them from others. However, remnants of this culture still persist among young Hispanic and Asian-American Catholics. Cultural families have significant influence on the religiosity of young people, and yet the overwhelming economic and social forces that are created today push young adults toward a more dominant secular culture that defines religion in therapeutic, evangelical Protestant, or consumerist manners. These young adults find solace in getting direction from others—a sense of emotive prayer styles and experiences and a kind of brand-name respectability on several fronts.

Candice is no different. While she attended Catholic schools from grammar school through high school, Candice really built "a foundation on Christ and the moral tenets of the church" at her high school run by the Benedictine monks.

Her spirituality is an emotive one. Sometimes it is touching and sometimes it is filled with rage. She gets moved to tears when she sings in the choir, an experience she remembers happening to her since she was a child singing in the children's choir. *"I really felt the presence of the Holy Spirit, so much so that I would be moved to tears. I used to feel like if I'm praying and I'm not moved, then there's something wrong. I had to learn that you don't love God for how he makes you feel; you love God for who he is. So if you're praying it's like any relationship. Sometimes it's good and sometimes it's bad. Of course it's great when you are moved by prayer—it's refreshing! It reminds you of why you believe what you believe. But in times when you don't feel any-thing, it's a real test of faith to decide how you're going to react to those times. What do you do? Do you dismiss it? Do you go back and pray again? When I don't "feel prayer," I simply dismiss my prayer and simply say, 'I'll talk to you later.' I think sometimes when I don't feel it; I have to reevaluate what I'm asking for or what I am thinking or even just the overall situation."*

One of those situations came just as Candice was heading off to college at the University of Illinois. *"My brother and sister were diagnosed with a visual impairment called stargardts, in which they are basically legally blind. I was really upset. I'm not sure if I was upset with God or what, but it was really difficult for me to see them suffer. They needed to use large-print books, and quite often they couldn't see the board in school. It just made me mad, and I didn't know where to turn. I had all these emotions and didn't know what to do. So when I went to college, I didn't really turn away from the church, but I had it on the back burner. I thought a good way to grow in my faith was to become a eucharistic minister and see what I could do through church, at least while I was in school, as I had been doing throughout my life. Because church had always been part of my life, it stayed that way."*

One of the things that Candice longs for still is structure. As a Millennial young adult Candice has come to enjoy the rhythms of a structured life. Going back to her childhood, Candice's mother had a very structured home. *"I'm not sure if this is just typical of Asian families, but my mom would write out a whole schedule for me for each day. It would be in fifteen-minute or half-hour or hour increments, depending on the activity, like 'eat a snack at 3:00 until 3:30' and 'at 4, practice piano until 5.' There was no downtime. And I guess my prayer life is a lot like that. I see a spiritual director, and she leads me through this structure where she tells me that on the first week we're going to do 'x' and the next week we're going to do 'y.' We're going to learn how to read the Bible and learn methods of praying. I know not all directors work this way, but I think that this did provide me with some guidance and discipline which, for me, was necessary, I think."*

At her university's Newman Center, Candice attended Mass and occasionally served as a eucharistic minister, but felt like she was always outside the community looking in.

"Mass was always something very personal and individualistic for me. When I saw people worshiping and praising together I really found that to be a strong physical manifestation of God. Not that I wasn't in my own way, it's just that I didn't really want to be part of a community. Often I think I was angry at God in personal prayer because of what happened to my siblings, so I didn't want to join a community that seemed to be so happy about God. I'm a happy person, but when I saw people hugging one another and greeting one another I felt like maybe I wasn't a happy person in my faith because often I was angry with God."

There was a retreat that people were always raving about called Koinonia, and people were constantly telling Candice that she should try it. *"I think I was a bit reluctant to go during my first three years of college because I was scared that perhaps I wasn't the good Catholic that God wanted me to be. Other folks seemed to be, at least on the surface, better Catholics, while others seemed to be very engaged in the community while I was still on the outside."* Finally a close friend of Candice's went on the

Koinonia retreat and encouraged her to attend. When she finally made that leap, she was incredibly surprised by the experience.

"I learned that everyone struggles in their relationship with God. I think I misinterpreted people's actions and expressions at Mass. The retreat was a big turning point in my life. I felt like I could start growing in my relationship with God. I had a relationship with God, but it tended to be an angry one. Now I started to realize that God has his own reasons, and I needed to let go and let God. I was finally able to open myself up and not be so angry at God anymore. I began to feel like a part of the community, and I think I felt more accepted by them. I really thought that because I had an angry relationship with God that they wouldn't accept me."

Candice makes a valid point here. A strong welcome is always a necessary part of any vibrant faith community, but many times even in a very vibrant community, some lost people stay lost. It is easy to be anonymous in a church, and sometimes the lost really want and need to be found by another. One of the struggles in parish life is that we meet people that we like and become friends with, and then we exclude ourselves from the rest of the community. If there is no intentional welcome, it is easy for us to simply "preach to the choir." The prevailing attitude needs to be one of welcome and engagement with strangers without being overbearing. (Chapter 5 will consider this further.) Candice made the mistake of equating friendliness with piety, an easy misconception to make, but certainly her parish could have engaged her better. After all, she was already a eucharistic minister. Perhaps she may have been shy or withdrawn or may have sent out bad body language signals, but we merely cannot preach to the converted. We need to seek out those who might not immediately engage themselves in our community in order to make those people feel more welcome or secure. In doing this, we enable them to have the freedom to pray as they need—whether that's in a private sense or a more communal one.

Retreat ministry tends to be a significant hallmark in the outreach process for both Generation X and Millenials. So it is not surprising that Candice resonated with her experience on retreat. I recently met Candice on one of my retreats and she contributed significantly in many ways. As the youngest participant, Candice provided the group with a unique perspective, and yet her experiences resonated with others older than herself. While perhaps more traditional and evangelical in her faith, Candice takes care in being respectful of others who are on a spiritual search, giving them room to navigate their feelings for themselves.

The second intersection for the two generational groups is the need for a nonjudgmental community. We see here that in Candice's Newman Center community judgments can be made even nonverbally. Certainly the group had a strong sense of welcome, but yet Candice struggled to connect with anyone in the group in a deep manner. In many ways she felt different from the others, and yet in the retreat setting, much of that melted away. It makes intuitive sense as Candice mentions, *"I realized that people on a retreat were probably the least likely to judge me because they know that you're there to change in some way, to reconnect with faith."*

Even in communities that might tend toward exclusivity, seekers need to realize that the extremes in any community are usually not in the majority but are often characteristic of a vocal minority. Candice found this to be the case when she was at Illinois. *"Some people were very fanatical, and I respected that, but I felt that that just wasn't me. And I think there were some who were reluctant to join the community because of that. But once you realize that community is much more than the 'super Catholics,' you see a wide range of people involved, and that's true of any group. I mean about a thousand people have gone on these retreats and yes, you'll find those super Catholics but you'll also find other people that are from other points on the spectrum."*

Another point is well taken here. There is a tendency to identify ministry groups by the appearance of the strong personality of just a few of its members. This is like judging a book by its cover. The one thing we should remember is the overwhelming diversity among young adults. So the Bacik/Reese identifications are paramount in keeping us grounded in our judgments. Young adults are in every flavor in all of our parishes, so our outreach must also remain varied and not single-minded in its approach.

While tradition contributed much toward the meaning behind her actions, Candice knows that *"tradition helps and guides me because I'm human and I'm going to err, so the tradition and direction help me overcome the things that I'm not supposed to believe in."* Candice is what I would term a private evangelical (perhaps the Catholic equivalent of being spiritually schizophrenic?), someone who expresses faith quietly but is deeply moved when she expresses it openly. It is a profound faith that she has slowly become unafraid to share with others and cannot help but express it through song, mentoring, deep contemplation, and yes, even tears. What more could one ask for from God?

Profile 2: Brooke T., Twenty-five, Catholic High School Teacher, Ohio/New York

Brooke T. grew up in what she terms "a very conservative, evangelical fundamentalist section of Ohio," where her family was one of the few Catholic families in the area. She attended public schools, and her CCD classes were only attended by five kids.

"Everyone was Protestant! We were the weird kids. While CCD was a good experience in defining what being Catholic was all about, I really saw myself as a Christian because of the influence of all these evangelical Protestant groups around me."

Brooke was involved in many types of nondenominational groups, from a Bible camp to mission trips. Even when she chose to attend a Catholic college at the University of Dayton, Brooke's friends were still mostly Protestants, and she would attend their services.

"To me it seemed no different going to Mass than going to a service in a Methodist Pentecostal church. I didn't get involved in the local campus ministry very much. I would do some things with the Catholic campus ministry, but most of the time I was part of a nondenominational group."

It was her participation in a mission trip with this nondenominational group that led Brooke back to her Catholic roots. *"When I went on this mission trip over the summer, I went to Mass only once throughout the entire summer, and it was then that I realized that I missed going to Mass and what it meant to be Catholic. I thought going on the mission trip might lead me to consider leaving the Catholic Church, but that summer really changed things for me. Being Catholic was important to me after all."*

The mission trip took place in South Carolina at Myrtle Beach and consisted of young people "witnessing for Christ." Brooke notes, *"When I think about it now, it's embarrassing how we would just walk up to people, especially young adults…and be up front about asking 'What do you think about God?' and really getting them to the point that they understand who God is, so that they can be saved and know Jesus as their personal savior. We would even just walk up to people randomly. So I look at it now, and it was so intrusive and judgmental in a lot of ways. Once I did a trip over spring break in Panama City, and there would be some people who'd be drunk and would get engaged with us in conversation. They'd be like, 'Yeah, I used to be Christian but I* guess I've fallen away,' so it worked to an extent. The numbers of people we brought in were always highlighted, and it was sort of 'capitalist driven.' How many numbers can you get? It totally screwed up my life in thinking about how God works, you know, in thinking about whether or not you were saved."

Brooke has come to embrace the idea about how young people see God much in the same ways as they see the Google search engine working. "I see this with my students now. They want to google something and then they take the first thing that they find and say, 'Well this must be the truth, and it gives me the answer that makes me feel happy.' I think that's what I saw with the whole evangelizing thing. It gave me immediate gratification, but it didn't leave room for the area where life isn't so black and white, and that's why my Catholicism became more important. There are so many layers and things are so interwoven, and you can't always separate them so easily, and it's OK to not always know the right answer. Not that you give up and don't try to seek the truth or stop living the gospel message, but that sometimes the dark times of life can be heartbreaking and the mystery that exists is that we never can completely know God. Catholicism isn't like Times Square, where everything is very artificial and bright lights make things clear. While that's fascinating, there's a softer, much more beautiful side to Catholicism that's so rich, and I think that it would take more than a lifetime to completely know all there is or has been said about God. Our tradition is so rich, and I never experienced that when I was doing more of the nondenominational things."

Brooke longed to rest in tradition during her mission trip but found the ritualistic sense of her nondenominational group lacking. "It was ridiculous—we didn't even go to church every Sunday, and we were supposed to be doing God's work! Having Bible study at night was great, but I really wanted to go to Mass. So I took a guy with me who was Protestant, and he just wanted to see what it was like. We ended up having to sit in the choir *loft and I could barely hear, but I knew I missed this. When I told the others that I had been to Mass, they weren't offensive about it but it started this debate about Catholicism among us, with people saying that my church was teaching things that were erroneous and Catholics aren't willing to stand up for their faith. That got me angry and I realized that I wanted to be Catholic, so I started going to Mass as soon as I got back to campus."*

On the cusp of both the Millennial and Gen X mindsets, Brooke is a good mixture of both groupings. She longs for tradition in order to have a sense of history and order. Her religion is not a one-hit wonder that was created out of the blue, but rather has a long and storied tradition filled with people whose shoulders she can stand on, and takes solace in the fact that her religion has stood the test of time in many ways.

When ritual was wanting, the familiar rhythms of the Mass became something to be treasured in Brooke's eyes. *"When I returned to Mass at my college for the first time I remember it being the most boring thing on the face of the planet. The homily was boring and some guy was asking for money, but I really think that it was one of the most—and I don't have this experience very often—beautiful moments for me spiritually. The ritual itself, the beauty of the church, the Eucharist being there, and seeing all of it steeped in this mystery led me to some vision of what God is."*

Longing for a more traditional mindset in a faith experience, Brooke joined a group of what she terms "about ten ultra-conservative Catholics." Like her nondenominational experience, the group believed in universal truths where "this is right and this is wrong," Brooke said. *"It wasn't all bad. We prayed the rosary and learned about saints and did adoration often. But there was no appreciation for the depth and the mystery of the tradition. You simply wore Catholicism on your sleeve, but it didn't seem very authentic or organic. It was very rigid and revolved*

*around trying to make something happen as opposed to allow-
ing it to grow."*

This is a typical experience of many young adults with
whom I have ministered. Often we find that many Millennial
young adults long to know the tradition of Catholicism, but that
longing doesn't stop merely with knowing the history of sin.
Millennial young adults want to know how church teaching
developed. They want to know the richness of diversity within
our tradition and how we have been able to discern what the
church has come to hold as true over the centuries. Catholicism
is not and has never been a static and unchanging tradition. It
has, however, continued to express wisdom rather well, with the
best minds of every age contributing much to its thought. How
we unfold that tradition for young people is crucial.

Brooke is just one young adult who has been fortunate
enough to have mentors and colleagues who were able to walk
with her on the road to reforming meaning in her life. During
graduate school at Fordham, Brooke was faced with her first spiritual crisis in which the presuppositions she had come to believe
as true were shattered.

*"I thought grad school was going to ruin me. I mean, reli-
gion is so wrapped up in who you are as a person, and so when
I started to hear and read the different takes within the church
that people had on God and Christ and the different doctrines
of the church...those were earth shattering. It was breaking all
of the boundaries that I had set up. Truth had become so static,
and everything had an absolute answer, and if you deviate from
that you're going to hell and that's the end. I don't think this
experience opened me up to relativism, but rather that God is a
lot bigger than I had been giving God credit for and that while
now I'm happy to have had that experience, before I started it
had terrified me. I literally cried."*

It was taking time to talk with professors and especially with
other students her own age that helped Brooke navigate her way

to a more informed faith that grew and became far stronger than she expected.

"Some students were very comfortable with having their ideas of God stretched in that way. Some of them had already been through that, but some of us had never been through that and were like...this is insane...this is terrifying. I think the more we learned and experienced, not just academically but also in our own personal spiritual lives, and even in prayer experiences within the school, slowly but surely, for me it was a process of letting go of what I had assumed and allowing myself to learn from other people. I also learned that others have vastly different experiences than I do, but that doesn't mean that they're wrong entirely. I think that was the biggest help."

While in graduate school, outside of the intellectual faith community that she had formed, Brooke looked to develop a faith community while living in a suburb of New York City. *"I basically tried to find other young people to hang out with at a local church. I wanted to find someone at church who was not forty-five with a family or eighty and in the rosary altar society, and the closest I came to finding this was the priest at my parish who was probably thirty-two or thirty-three. So I would talk to him a lot but it was like...well, it's me and the priest! I would see other young adults in the parish, but they never seemed like they wanted to be engaged. I tried to join the choir, but they were all older people, and I just didn't feel this connection to be part of a parish. I didn't want to be the token young person."*

Here is where the largest challenge to any parish lies. As a young adult ministry lobbyist, I often hear from pastors that they would like to be able to provide young adult ministry activities for people, but the demographic just does not seem to be present in their parish. Those that *are* present seem to be ambivalent about joining any such group within the parish structure. Many parish staffs lack a vibrant sense of evangelization that looks beyond the parish walls, boundaries that have little meaning to the average young adult. We want young adults to be part of our community, but then we play a bait and switch. We welcome them into communities where there is little life and very few people like them.

Brooke was asked by a priest friend to start a young adult group in her parish under his direction. He tempered some of her enthusiasm for a wide-ranging social justice ministry and instead started with some simple social activities that drew about fifteen people on a regular basis. The group did not grow beyond the social activities, and when it eventually started dwindling, five men and Brooke became the core members of the group. *"It was very frustrating with five guys and me! The social stuff wasn't working, and I ended up merging the group with a group from another parish but again, the group was really superconservative, where everyone was trying to find immediate answers instead of exploring faith together and trying not to be judgmental of others."* In short, the group was not attracting any new people, but instead chose to form their own exclusive Catholic ghetto where faith was not reformed but rather regressed. The theology of the immediate answer took precedence over the dark night of the soul and a search for truth. Those in the group felt that they had the truth already and weren't about to let anyone into the group that might allow that feeling to waver.

This group needed mentors who could help those seeking traditional piety to practice in a traditional way alongside those who were searching to simply figure out where they were in terms of a personal faith. At the same time, evangelical and sacramental young adults need to continue in their education and faith development as well. The formation of faith is a lifetime journey and not a quick-fix approach. We never hold the truth of our faith as absolute certainty. This is what makes faith such a risk. Without risk, faith ceases to exist. Instead, as Karl

Rahner would say, "God is the inexhaustible one; the question which has no answer."[1] The tendency among more pious young adults may be to have an exclusivist version of faith. It is always a recipe for disaster to allow this mentality to become the prevailing wisdom in a young adult group.

At the same time, there needs to be a prevalent Catholic identity. Groups often swing too far the other way, in which all things are open to interpretation and the teachings of the church are simply thrown to the wind. What is it in the wisdom of our tradition that we have come to believe is always true, and why do we believe that in faith? We do not know absolutely if these things are true; rather they are the best expressions of truth that the church has discerned over two thousand years. This is certainly not something to be taken lightly. At the same time it provides young adults with room to question the tradition, to criticize our beliefs, and to try on doctrines of faith and measure them vis-à-vis with their experiences in the culture. As church, we also need to be responsive to the wisdom that young people have garnered from the modern culture in which they are immersed. We need to point out the wisdom in what they have found there and criticize what we believe is flawed based on the teachings of two thousand years of tradition. What do other traditions say that we hold valuable and how do they challenge our own ideas? This is all fair game for young adults. Most often, though, the process of critical examination lacks effectiveness or gets muddied in poor translations that end up giving short shrift to church teachings. (Part 3 will explore this in greater depth.)

Brooke is a good example of how ministry often loses people in translation. *"I never heard of Catholic social teaching until I went to college. There was definitely always a sense of praying for people and hearing about their life stories and hoping that this would compel us to be better people. But in my non-denominational college group people talked about knowing*

Jesus and who had the longest time in prayer that day. Meanwhile, I would see the consumption and materialism and the lack of concern for issues that were happening in our own country and around the world! I didn't think that made any sense." In ministry, though, not many directly link Catholic social teaching to service projects or to an outreach among the poor. These are simply nice examples of Christian charity. Although most religions may have these tenets within their various denominations, Catholicism has a rich history of social doctrines that is inherent in the faith tradition. Scores of documents have been written and yet they often go unread. For years, people said that Catholic social teaching was the church's best kept secret. Many people who minister with young adults often speak about Catholic social teaching as being a constitutive element of Catholicism, but they do not point to any specifics. They merely mention those three magic words: Catholic social teaching. In short, we have so many great examples of people living out Catholic social teaching, but no one who takes the time to effectively translate the wisdom it is based upon within Catholic tradition. In a world of information overload we need to provide these references quickly and simply in memorable sound bytes that can be easily consumed by a hungry audience that feeds on solid tradition.

Brooke also struggles with her prayer life as a Millennial. *"Often, I was really trying to have a more ritualistic approach toward prayer. I was doing the rosary a lot and adoration, but I hadn't been raised with that. I didn't have any direction and just thought that the rosary and adoration were the holier things to do instead of journaling or talking to God. I was praying blind!"* Brooke came away without a preference for adoration and the rosary but an assumption that these prayer practices worked without fail; that these were, by default, better ways to pray. Nobody mentored her in finding out what ways of praying allowed her to change for the better. Instead, Brooke pounded her head against the wall trying to pray "the right way."

"My prayer life is up and down, honestly. I would love to say that I set aside five minutes each day to just be quiet; that was my New Year's Resolution this year—to do that—but sometimes it has to take place when I'm walking. So that means taking the headset off or trying to have that time to be quiet. But I think prayer opens my heart more in that I don't ask God for things, but rather, I look at what I really need to work on, who do I need to be open to interacting with. That's been the primary force in my idea of grace: how I need to try to be like Christ and trying to love, and that takes place in very different forms in my prayer life, whether I journal, or I'm just being silent, or listening to meditative music, or reading something and getting away from the idea that God is related only to those forms that are explicitly religious. Like being in a church, or reading the Bible or a spiritual book— I think I now try to see God in all things. I think that's what going to a graduate school at a Jesuit institution did for me.

"I still go to Mass. I go because it's a deliberate way for me to give some time to God alone…it's the one part of the week that's just about God. I don't do the rosary regularly unless I'm doing it with my students, but I still like to do adoration. I like the silence of it and the idea that I'm forcing myself to be in that presence and realizing that the Eucharist is what binds us as a community of people, whether it's the pious types or someone whom I saw in a bar the night before, because Christ wants all of us and that's a beautiful experience.

"I still go to reconciliation every two months or so just because the rhythm of it is beautiful and not just because it unburdens me of my sins, but because I'm really able to experience God through that sacrament in a different way than I do in my everyday life. This time is specifically holy. I need to be reminded that I'm vulnerable; I'm a woman and not God. I know

that it's uncomfortable to confess my sins to a man, being a woman and all, but I need that vulnerable moment to remind me of that."

In short, Brooke longed for an adult sense of faith, one that held water with both the wisdom of her experience and the wisdom of two thousand years of the experience of the church. She hoped to find a tradition she could be proud of, with rhythms in that tradition that touched her soul in deep and meditative ways.

Brooke feels that *"there are areas I need to work on. I'm learning more now, especially because I work for the church as a Catholic school teacher. I'm trying to learn to separate between being angry at people in the church and allowing myself to appreciate the treasures that the church has to offer. Everything from the sex abuse scandal to people who think because we're a Catholic school we shouldn't admit students to the school who aren't Catholic because we have a Catholic identity to uphold. First of all, we'd probably have five students left! It makes me angry that there are people in the church who have that attitude. So I struggle with people who have that attitude and try not to judge them and realize that they have an experience that they are terrified to let go of, like I was in grad school. Maybe this is what gives them consistency. It angers me because I have seen that turn off many people who are my age and the teens I work with as well. They are not allowed to have a really honest experience of Catholicism."* Brooke's God is an honest God, one she's not going to fool and one who constantly surprises her. In the simple moments of each day Brooke is able to discern what is of God, and while she longs for moments in which the echoes of traditional ritual resonate with her heart, she knows that God is never simply mired in these moments of liturgical beauty. Rather, it is each moment of daily living that Brooke has come to see as charged with the grandeur of God.

Profile 3: Julia T., Twenty-two, Fordham University Student, Washington, DC/ New York City

Julia is a clear-cut Millennial young adult who has had many profound liturgical experiences in the church, and that has been her primary exposure, as a Sunday Catholic and a lifelong Catholic school student. *"As a child we attended Holy Trinity Church in Washington, DC. They had an amazing 9:30 a.m. family Mass. The music was wonderful. They used drums and guitars, and during the closing hymn all the children jingled their parents' keys to the beat. Each priest had a different 'gimmick.' One priest used a hand puppet; another, known as the "drawing priest," would draw beautiful illustrations of the gospel during his homily. Looking back, the great thing about this Mass was that it was entertaining for children and parents. We still go now, but a lot of those priests have left, and it's not really the same."*

Julia clearly shows aspects of the social young adult and even bleeds over into the evangelical camp without being conservative. She has a sense of liturgy that mixes between sensual experience and a love for the communal life. Cautiously, one wonders if liturgy for her is or has been little more than entertainment. Julia interned at my office this past semester, and I think she was able to explore her spiritual side a bit more than she previously had. She spoke to me about boring high school liturgy, although she connected well with the monthly ritual of the sacrament of reconciliation.

"It wasn't until I started going to Fordham [a Jesuit school in New York City] that I began to reconnect with my faith. I was extremely homesick, and I decided to go to the university church and pray one night. I was the only one there. The next week my friend Stephanie asked me if I wanted to go to the Sunday night

Mass, and I've been going ever since. At first I was just trying to be somewhere that felt like home, but I started to listen and realized I was praying on my own all the time, and now I never miss it. The homilies at Fordham are usually aimed at under-graduates, and there is a great community feel because I usually at least recognize everyone there."

Yet another mix of Millennial and Gen X longings is exemplified with Julia. Julia obviously has had a wonderful home life, a life that she evidently missed when she headed from Maryland to New York City for college. At this time of transition, church was the only place that felt like "home." It became a good family, nurturing both togetherness and personal development. For Julia, church was the surrogate, not for a tangible family but for the feelings of security that the recalling of family and religious ritual provided for her. It is one of the beautiful things about the Catholic faith.

However, what did the ritual provide her with spiritually outside of that familial recollection? Julia states, *"I think for the most part I see my faith as a very personal relationship with God. That being said, I think we are all connected, and as Catholics we have an obligation and a privilege to accept every-one with empathy and understanding. Globally, we will never begin to move in the right direction unless world leaders/policy makers look at all of humanity as an 'us' that we are all respon-sible for. There is so much 'us versus them' alongside this unde-fined 'other' that creates injustice and prejudice. Desmond Tutu has a lot of great things to say about our situation in terms of a general selfishness and combativeness that are running the world. He has often said that our only hope is to have women run the world. I think I agree with him."*

Again, clearly it is a social dimension that predominates here in Julia's spirituality, and yet it seems that the ritual has given her a new sense of the sacramental nature of the world. Julia sees what many of us do not, that Jesus Christ, who we come to know through the Eucharist, is also alive and well in the world, and all we need to do is look to those who need empathy and understanding to find him. Julia notes, *"I see God in different people and in the experiences I have all the time."*

A strong feminist, Julia notes, *"Even when I was not particularly active in my faith [Julia had a rather rebellious adolescence], I have always seen God as a kind of mother figure. I know a lot of people say he is a father figure, but I am extremely close with my mother, and most of the closest relationships in my life are with women. I believe, above all, God wants me to be happy. Like my relationship with my mother, this means setting down rules sometimes. That being said, God to me is pure unconditional love, and when I look at different things I believe go against that relationship, I always find that whatever I am struggling with is also hurtful to me in some way. I don't think any of God's expectations of me are arbitrary, but for my own good. So many times I have been let down to later find out that everything happened for a greater reason."*

Julia also prefers some of the quiet contemplation that private young adults long for. She found that working at Busted Halo.com has *"made my faith even stronger, and it's a direct result of contemplating the issues we actively discussed in editorial meetings and reading different articles on the site."*

Like most young adults, personal everyday experience is largely linked with her faith life. At times it marks the intersection of ambiguity for Julia. *"One place in my life that I have questioned God's presence is with regard to my best friend, Kelly. I have known her since I was seven years old, and she is the most amazing person in my life. Kelly has struggled with virtually every issue a young girl in her position can encounter. She has been near death from anorexia and bulimia, tried to end her own life in high school, and has been on antidepressants for years. This is the closest thing in my life to a disaster that I have experienced personally. Even though some people have told me she is choosing to do this to herself, there is nothing voluntary about her problems. I honestly can't say I've resolved the issues I have with her sickness and how God figures in. I pray for her a lot, and I can only hope that one day, like the other disappointments I have experienced, I will look back and see a lesson in all of it for both of us. Thinking about this situation, I see God in her on a daily basis."*

Julia wastes no time in pointing out where she most struggles with the church as well: *"Most of the issues I have with the church are due to its stance on sexuality. All of these arguments have been stated a million times before, and I agree with a lot of others who have said that if Jesus were here today, he would not have condemned homosexuality."*

Other issues such as abortion and premarital sex are not as easy to write off: *"I am personally pro-life, but I think the social ramifications of outlawing abortion would be horrific. Women would resort to going to unlicensed doctors, and some would be kicked out of their families. No issue is black and white, and abortion is no exception."* While Julia struggles with these teachings she has no desire to leave the church, but rather to grapple with them from within. She often argues that the church offers no guidelines for young adults on sexuality other than not doing it.

"In regard to premarital sex, I think sex is an important part of any relationship and should be figured out before you make a lifetime commitment. In this instance I have to have faith in my relationship with God, and I personally believe after a lot of prayer and contemplation that sexuality is a part of my life and that I can in good conscience reconcile this with my spirituality."

So while Julia doesn't echo the church's views on sexuality and perhaps hasn't examined many of the church's writings on the subject (such as John Paul II's *Theology of the Body*), she does seem to exhibit a love for the Catholic faith. She loves the rhythm of ritual and the community around her throughout it.

She has a very sensitive concern for the poor of the world and for the injustices that women face, both here and abroad. All are extremely Catholic positions. Perhaps the goal for someone like her, for a young adult minister, would be to guide her toward some of the more profound writings on sexuality and also help her to examine and contrast where the church and modern science agree and are at odds. In my own life as a young adult I have come to appreciate the church's position on many such issues after careful investigation. However, I believe that Julia has come up with some valuable insights. Young adults believe that there is not only wisdom within the church's viewpoint but that wisdom also can be found in their community and in the life experiences that teach them things firsthand. Perhaps there is room in our church for both, and perhaps that is what young adults most long for.

Profile 4: Linda I., Twenty-five, Community Organizer, Arizona

Linda grew up as the oldest of nine children of her Mexican mother and Nigerian father in the hot Arizona sun. Catholicism in this diverse family was the common bond that united her parents' distinct cultures and also allowed the individuality of her siblings and her to come together in unity around a common ritual.

Linda notes, *"We didn't necessarily grow up going to church every Sunday. We would go if my grandparents were around; then we'd go quite often [laughs]...but definitely on the big holidays. All the kids were baptized and made sacraments. My parents always talked about God very openly at home, so that was always there even if we didn't go to church every single Sunday."*

While Linda went to public school mostly because of the large expense of sending nine children to a private school, her faith remained strong. The Mexican neighborhood she grew up in was also ripe with Catholic ritual and celebration. With Immaculate Conception, Our Lady of Guadalupe's feast day, and Christmas, December was filled with religious fervor, as if Christmas lasted all month. Culturally, Linda felt the Catholic flavor all over the place. Her family was Catholic, and it was ingrained in the rhythms of her neighborhood, but generally speaking faith didn't take a firm grasp on her until her senior year of high school.

Linda notes: *"It was all because of my little sister. While faith in our family was always there, but just in the background, we didn't really think about it too much. It was simply who we were. But my sister's best friend is Mormon, and she started to talk to her about church and started going to services with her. And then she started to consider becoming Mormon. Which, well...let's just say was a little family crisis. But my parents knew that my sister was very stubborn. So they knew that if they said no to her, she would just be more obstinate about converting. So they said, 'If you want to convert to Mormonism, then you have to research Mormonism.'"*

Linda continued her story with great fervor and respect for her sister's searching: *"So off went my sister to read books written by people who were Mormon, by people who had left the Mormon church, and by others who weren't Mormon. When she finished reading all this stuff she said, 'I do not want to be Mormon; I'm so glad I'm Catholic!'"*

The wisdom of her parents' plan awakened a religious longing in their daughter, and Linda gravitated toward that exploration of faith as well. *"Then [my sister] was more interested in doing things like going to daily Mass. She began to drag the entire family to church every morning! And for some strange reason, we would all go—including my parents! I'm not sure why, but we did. So I started taking my faith more seriously because she started taking it more seriously. And she started reading more books about Catholicism and would pass them on to me."*

For Linda the search didn't stop there. After entering Northern Arizona University, Linda began to take more ownership of her own faith. *"My roommate was Lutheran but was really more of a fundamentalist Baptist in her practice, and she strongly identified herself as a Christian. She led a Bible study and was very much into her faith. I love the girl and was in her wedding and all, but back then she started questioning me about what I believed. I had never been asked what I believe, and even though I had read some books, I never had to defend what I believed before!"*

Linda's life up until college consisted of being around strong Catholics. Now her environment had shifted to involve experiences with people of other faiths, including her roommate. She took on the challenge of defending her faith with conviction, only to find her arsenal bare. She notes, *"I even got into some arguments with people at my friend's church [which she would occasionally attend with her roommate], but I found that I couldn't support my arguments as well as they could. So that was a big dilemma for me. At this point in my life I hadn't been confirmed, so I decided to go to confirmation classes at the Newman Center. I figured the whole point of confirmation classes was to see if I even wanted to be Catholic. However, I still went to my roommate's church as well because while I always have the feeling that it is like home for me in the Catholic Church, her church was more evangelical and very vibrant, which was something I hadn't experienced before. I had never been part of a church where I had been an active member. It was more of a 'just go in and sit there and listen' experience before. So her church was very cool and different, but I would still go to Mass in the morning and then her church service in the evening."*

The highlight of Linda's confirmation classes was being able to be free on the search. Nothing seemed to be out of bounds for her campus ministry to explore. They valued her searching and gave her both the wisdom of Catholic tradition and enough space to discern the questions she had about Catholicism. Linda calls these classes "life altering" and notes that she *"learned so much and I'm so glad I did this in college because that's when I felt really free to question and research a lot of the stuff behind the teachings. I had a great campus minister who totally pushed us to question, and he was so well informed himself. It was a really good environment to be in. So by the time I finished with the classes I had very firmly decided to be confirmed and to stay Catholic, and I felt like I had many more reasons why. It wasn't just that being Catholic felt right, but now I had some intellectual knowledge of what I believe. I knew why I disagreed with the people from my roommate's church, and now I could argue with them."*

Linda found a great core group of friends at the Newman Center, and that changed everything. *"Those friends are still my close girlfriends today. I became an intern at the Newman Center and got very involved. While hanging out at that Newman Center I first heard about the Jesuit Volunteer Corps totally by accident! We heard that someone from JVC was coming and that there was free pizza. So of course we went! I was literally just there for the food! But I was intrigued by the program and how well it seemed to be running. I knew that I wanted to continue to be involved in the church. I felt called to do something that contributed to others directly, especially to people who were less economically empowered. The funny thing is that the only reason JVC stops there is because it's on the way to California and it's a convenient stop for their recruiting team in Flagstaff. So each time they came I would go and listen, and it would build up my interest."* It seemed like a natural fit for Linda, who also found her love for social justice, chairing her college's community service program. She remembers, *"I had a great interest in global issues, so we tended to do a lot of fasts and walks to raise money for Operation Rice Bowl."*

After college Linda joined JVC but didn't really understand that there were theological differences among orders of priests. The Jesuits were certainly different from the priests she grew up with but, after coming off this huge faith growth experience in college, Linda was looking for something that would take her deeper into her faith. She was in for somewhat of a rude awakening.

"It was very comfortable and very normal for me to talk about God with my friends. I mean we'd go over to a friend's house and we'd just have a Bible study. In JVC spirituality is one of the four core things, and after all, it's the Jesuit Volunteer Corps, so I kind of expected it to be the same. But what I found was quite the opposite. I lived with seven other people, and I found that a lot of my roommates were just sort of indifferent to faith. So that was really confusing and frustrating because I felt like I was the crazy Christian in the group. I was probably the one who went most consistently to Mass, and I would bring up God or things in conversation. It was very different for me to be the one who was most radical in that sense. They were all great people, don't get me wrong, but it was just a very different experience for me."

As Linda lived in the house, providing help at a community organizing office, she struggled a bit spiritually in the midst of her newfound household. *"We had to have a community night and a spirituality night every week, and we actually kept up with it. But when I planned the spirituality nights I would want to read from scripture and when someone else would plan it they would just want to take a walk. So I tended to be more traditional. They [her roommates] also never had to defend their faith before, and I think this was a good thing, so I also knew a lot more in a sense, because they had just been around Catholics most of their life [much like Linda herself was in college]. A lot of them had some criticisms of the Catholic Church, and of course I have my own criticisms of the church or things I just didn't agree with, but they had some very strong criticisms that I hadn't heard before, so I think it was really interesting to be in this kind of environment. Several of the criticisms were really well founded, and I agreed with some of them. However, some were simply because they felt the church was overbearing, and this was their way of lashing out or rebelling. So I wondered why they had chosen JVC instead of Americorps!"*

Perhaps what Linda was looking for most was mentorship, especially in the spiritual sense, and that is where she found the biggest problem with JVC's leadership. *"The leadership style was hands-off. I didn't think that God was really emphasized that much in JVC. By that I mean there was certainly a strong commitment to social justice but a lack of a faith component to social justice. I don't believe in social justice because I think it's nice or because it's the right thing to do, but rather because that's what I think we're called to do. I think it's 100 percent connected to God's plan for this world, and if it wasn't, I don't think I'd do it!"* Overall, Linda noted that there were some great parts of the spiritual experience. *"I have to say that they had retreats, and those were always pretty good. I mean, obviously there was a connection to Jesus as the one who initiated a lot of the steps of social justice, but I think they could've made more connections with the institutional church more often outside of the retreats because there's a lot of stuff on social justice in the catechism and in our tradition's history, but I still didn't know that when I left JVC. I had to do a lot of research after JVC on my own, and I still don't know that much because there's just so much out there and I haven't done all that much research."*

A typical Millennial, Linda has a strong regard for authority and tradition, yet she does not push her faith onto others or seem judgmental or exclusive about it. Rather, she simply looks for an opportunity to connect the wisdom of her tradition with the engagement of her social justice activities. This is a well-founded criticism by her in my opinion. Overall, Linda liked being part of JVC but still found that experience wanting in terms of connecting her actions to a faith tradition.

"I think what a lot of people did was make a connection with God. But even if you perceive these social justice principles to come from God, it doesn't mean that you see the Catholic Church as on board with that message. I didn't really get the connection that the church was a leader in social justice issues. And yet I know now that it is."

Linda stayed in New York following her JVC experience. But she *"hasn't really found a church in New York to be involved in. For me that's a big part of how I express my faith, so that's been kind of difficult. One of the things that I've had a really hard time with in the Catholic Church is a hesitation to kind of admit just how diverse the church is, especially in the United States. I mean if you look at the hierarchy, it's still a bunch of Caucasian men. Meanwhile a lot of lay people involved in the church are women, and I think it's starting to become women of color, and yet the hierarchy is still mostly white men."*

Linda wonders how parishes can be more representative of the congregation and does not tend to feel comfortable in one that does not keep that guiding principle at the fore. *"The church I attend now is OK; it's in this great cross section of Brooklyn, with people who speak Spanish and Haitian-Creole, and the pastor speaks all three languages [English obviously being the third]. Sometimes the Mass is trilingual. So I like the fact that when I go to Mass there are different kinds of families and different types of people culturally and ethnically, and when the pictures on the walls represent the community—the saints and everything, I can feel very comfortable."*

Still, diversity alone is not the only spiritual need for Linda. *"I don't really feel like I'm part of the community there. The parish tends to be people who have been members of the parish for some time. Everybody has grown up there, and there are a lot of families, so there aren't a lot of active young adult activities going on. So it's kind of just me as the lone single young adult, and I like to be involved in things that I believe in so I don't feel connected in that sense. I tried to be a lector, but I kept missing the dates they had scheduled for the lectors to be trained because I had to work during those times. I tried some other connections with the parish, but often I wouldn't hear back from them, so I'd eventually just give up. It's too bad. I've recently found a young adult group in Park Slope, and their events are pretty good, so I'm going to try to go to those more often to see what's going on there."*

Linda notes that, *"A lot of young adult events aren't very relaxed. I think I'm pretty laid back, and whenever I would go to the Theology on Tap events in Manhattan [run by a group that calls itself 'The Culture of Life' and has some backing from* Crisis *magazine and the Legionaries of Christ], everything was so intense, and I wanted to tell them to 'just RE-LAX.' Everyone was very confrontational, and I wanted to say, 'I believe the same things you do; you don't need to cram this down my throat. Chill out!' When I went to the Theology on Tap in Brooklyn, people were more relaxed, sitting on chairs. Things were a lot more in my vein."*

So Linda suffers from a parish that struggled to engage young adults within the confines of their parish roles and inquisition-like judgmental young adult groups that attack her faith before they have even come to know her. The Park Slope cluster of parishes in Brooklyn seems to be building young adult community events, but still, a single parish that she can call home is key for her sense of spirituality.

Still providing leadership in social justice, Linda has been able to integrate her spirituality into her everyday life. *"As I've gotten older, faith experiences are rarely faith experiences—you know—I love going to Mass and always have great experiences there, but it's rare that an intentional faith experience affects me. It's more when I have an experience in my everyday life that I reflect on later, usually with my family. When I reflect on those moments I realize that there was something bigger in those moments. A lot of hidden moments of God are there when I take the time to look."*

Perhaps the Jesuits taught her well after all, as this last note sounds a whole lot like the Ignatian Examen. When she looks back on her life so far, Linda celebrates the influence of her sister and college roommate:

"If they didn't believe so strongly...I wouldn't have been challenged to examine my own faith."

Profile 5: Jeff G., Twenty-four, Catholic Schoolteacher, New Orleans/New York City

On the cusp of Millennial young adulthood and Generation X sits Jeff G. Interestingly enough, he bucks the trend for the Millennials. *"My experience of the Catholic Church is largely one of community. This is why I keep coming back to church—because so many of my friends, heroes, and family members value the bond we share as Catholics. Of course, I would also say that I keep coming back because of the sacraments, most fundamentally the Eucharist. The Mass is essential to my experience of life. I really, really love the Mass."*

Jeff, a colleague and personal friend of mine, is clearly the odd mix that gives me hope. He has a clear viewpoint on both the vertical and horizontal bars of faith, meaning he has a strong sense that both community and a personal relationship with God are important for mature faith. Jeff, who has been part of many faith communities, has been profoundly influenced by his Jesuit education. He often attends daily Mass and is profoundly committed to Catholic education, serving as a high school teacher in an all-girls Catholic high school with mostly minority students. He views the Eucharist as an "intimate experience with Jesus" and yet does not have a very literal view of this, nor does he denigrate it to "theological magic." He views it as mystical experience that becomes profoundly real and tangible in a nonmystical way at the same time.

Jeff grew up as a military brat with two constants in his life: his family and the Catholic Church. Wherever Jeff's dad's Air Force career took them, he knew that the family would stick together and that church would continue to be part of his life. The Mass holds a precious place for him, most likely because of his past and his connection to it as something immutable. He notes: *"It's always the same liturgy; it was very comfortable to know that we'd have the same prayers and that this church culture would always be there no matter where we moved."*

Strangely enough, Jeff's religious life at home was not very deep, but a rather hum-drum commitment to a tradition.

"I think my family is more Catholic than they are religious. It's very important to them to say prayers, to be in Catholic school, and to go to Mass every Sunday. But if I had a question about something or a worry about something, Mom wouldn't say, 'Well, did you pray about that?' It's not like I observed my parents praying other than at formal things, like before meals, and it's not like we talked a lot about God. But the sense of Catholic culture as being something that we do—that happened a lot. The culture certainly created some of our moral values, you know, like 'do the right thing,' or 'be a person of service,' or 'be good to people'—those were important when I was a child. But

I don't remember my mom or dad saying directly to me that we do these things because we are Catholic."

Catholic school was another constant. Not only did Jeff attend Catholic schools since first grade, he also attended two different Jesuit high schools: one in Spokane, Washington, and Creighton Prep in Omaha, Nebraska. He later continued with the Jesuits at Loyola-New Orleans for college. He has been very influenced by the Jesuits and even more so by Ignatian spirituality. Jeff recalls, *"I think about Ignatius or Jesuit spirituality or something that a Jesuit taught me every day. Because I was so Jesuit minded, I decided to live with Dominicans for a year—during a year's service with Dominican volunteers. I knew so much about the Jesuits that I wanted to learn about another order. It actually taught me how 'Jesuit' [my spirituality] was. I saw that I perceived the world, as opposed to how Dominicans do, in a very Jesuit, or Ignatian way."*

Jeff's attraction to the Jesuits started when he was able to see that they had a commitment to things outside of the church and university doors. They had *"a real substantial commitment to social justice. Technically, all Jesuits believe in faith doing justice…but a few of them believe in it while teaching Latin in a posh university and maybe doing community service a few times a month. But the Jesuits that most inspired me, and the ones who made me think about being a Jesuit, were the ones who had that real commitment to social justice without making it a kind of totem. Ultimately, they were concerned about Jesus and about souls and the afterlife, but there's a real concern for the poor of this world now! I just fell in love with that."*

Perhaps more aptly stated, Jeff seemed also to abhor anything less than that kind of full commitment from others in the church. He noted frustration with a group called Compass, which is run by the Legionaries of Christ. *"I would go to these Compass meetings because one of my friends was involved [and later became the acting director of National College Compass], and there would be all this talk about saving souls and helping people, but there wasn't a lot of real institutional commitment to the poor or the marginalized—except for the sense that we need to pray. That's nice and all, and I don't mean to be flippant about it because that is obviously important, but I think we need to do more than just pray. At the same time, I'd have a hard time with superactivist Catholics too. I went to a meeting where activist Catholics were founding a group to create an alternative Catholic vision, a kind of social justice activism group, if you will. I remember asking at one of the meetings if could we pray before the meeting started. Everyone looked kind of uncomfortable, and someone said, 'I'm not sure about that.' I was like, 'Are you SERIOUS?! We're not going to pray before a meeting about Jesus!?' So while that sounds really trite and stereotypical and it's obviously more complicated than this, to some extent it's true. I found that people on the right don't often care about the poor and people on the left don't often care much about prayer. Now that's a bit oversimplistic because I think there are people who care about both from both sides—there's a lot more nuance to it than that. But if you want a really quick and dirty summary of the problem—I think that's it."*

Jeff, typical of Millennial Catholics in this way, often took an all-or-nothing approach to his Catholicism throughout college. He was going to be Catholic in both name and in deed. His experiences in both of the groups he found at Loyola fell well short of expectations.

"Compass was mostly about piety, personal salvation, eucharistic adoration, being devoted to Mary, the pope's theology of the body—the standard stuff. Which is fine. And those on the left would just talk about Gustavo Gutiérrez and Dan Berrigan and other social justice heroes."

So while mostly identifying with Catholics on the progressive side, Jeff was careful to stay grounded in a more traditional way of looking at things without going headlong into a full-on commitment with only being a sacramental or evangelical Catholic. Instead he sought balance, integrating the sacramental with the prophetic.

As time has passed, Jeff is able to note something profoundly true about young adult life in the church. *"This far left and far right Catholicism are the only things that people find attractive because they are the only things that offer any sense of rigor. I mean the Legionaires have tons of people in their seminary because they provide an alternative vision—which is sexy; it's cool to have an alternative vision. The Jesuits, at their best, also provide that, but the problem with a lot of Jesuit seminaries is that they promise this alternative vision because you have all these exciting Jesuits around, but when you get there you find middle-class complacency. I don't mean to be unfair to those Jesuits who are not middle-class complacent because there are plenty who are not, but I just know more than one person who has entered the Jesuit seminary and has been very disenchanted by their experience of seminary and their readings of Jesuit heroes like Pedro Arrupe or even St. Ignatius. I suppose the same could be said about any group in the Catholic Church itself. I mean how bad we all would look if we compared ourselves to Jesus! Or even Paul! The important thing to note is that there's this whole milquetoast Catholicism in the middle, which is like 80 or 90 percent of Catholics, and what they're looking for is not some sort of 'you can do your life any old way but just do it as a Catholic.' But rather, you can have a better life that's different and exciting and beautiful and meaningful in ways that it isn't now. And they want someone to show them how. If you try to simply tell people to 'do what you want but do it as a Catholic,' well, who cares!? I don't need to be Catholic anymore—I'm not afraid of going to hell! I'll just keep doing what I'm doing. I do things differently BECAUSE I'm Catholic."*

Jeff's life today continues to be shaped by a variety of religious communities. He's worked as an associate editor with the

Paulists at BustedHalo.com and presently teaches with the Sisters of St. Joseph. *"I also go to a church run by the Oratorians in Brooklyn, which is probably the best parish I've ever been to that's not a college parish. There's a real feeling of community. The music is unapologetically intellectual—very highbrow music, like Bach, or some kind of classical choir music—Russian composers whose names I never heard of before—it's beautiful. The choir director is not afraid to use his extensive training to give us beautiful music every week. That's the thing: Everything in this parish feels intentional—deliberate and thought out. I really appreciate that. Maybe because priests are overworked a lot, but I go to a lot of churches that feel mediocre or haphazard. But here, every Mass or every service is really impressive. And the homilies always sound practiced and well thought out and well considered. They're topical, relevant, often funny, smart without being pretentious...just really good! It's a good community for young people—I'm part of their young adult group. My first two years in New York I couldn't find any place like this one."*

As religious as Jeff is, he is also immersed in secular culture. As a teacher Jeff works upwards of seventy hours a week grading papers and taking on some extracurricular tasks with his students, like the yearbook. This creates a problem with his prayer life, or at least with the kind of prayer life he would like to have.

"In the summer I try to go to daily Mass or at least two to three times a week other than Sunday. Keeping a consistent prayer schedule is hard when you're working forty-hour weeks or even sixty-to-seventy-hour weeks. I think a lot of young people might have this problem; when you're working a forty-hour week or when you're in college and have a flexible schedule, prayer is a lot easier. But I work maybe sixty or seventy hours a week, maybe more, and I know people who work more. I don't know when they pray. I don't know when they ever could make time to pray. Yet I think I have a religiosity about my work—that I owe it to God to do

that work; I owe it to the people of God. Because it's not like I need this work just for me. I feel like the work I do is, at least to some degree, important. Teaching, service work, a doctorate one day… it's all good work…or at least I want it to be. That's why I do it."

When Jeff first moved to New York he brought that same fire he had for social justice in New Orleans with him. *"I was basically very ascetic. I had no clothes; I bought thrift-store clothes. I rarely got haircuts. I didn't go out to eat that often. And I wasn't even all that deliberate about it. I was just in an activist community who made this kind of faith-based commitment. I thought that we all needed to use our time and talents to make that happen. And I was pretty unforgiving to those that didn't in a way that I'm not now. I think I'm less impatient about all of that now."*

Jeff credits the melting pot that is New York as a place that enabled his faith to grow in new ways. *"One of the great things about moving to New York City was that I met a lot of rich people that I just wanted to hate for, you know, 'working for the man.' But instead I was really impressed by a lot of them because they were doing really good work. It became harder for me to think that if you're not working for a nonprofit or if you're not a full-time nun in prayer all day (I was OK with these people. I had some problems with people who prayed all day because I thought they should be doing more—and I was OK with artists, because we need beauty in the world.) then you were wasting your life. I had no respect for people in business."*

Jeff's radical lifestyle early on led him to bike across the country. *"We did a bike for life on the consistent ethic of life. The message was that all life is sacred and we need to radically change the way we live our lives, to be respectful of all life and have a commitment to all life. War was on the horizon, and we had just finished with the first Iraq war. It was then I felt like I was doing what priests were supposed to be doing—or maybe simply what Christians were supposed to be doing—going out there showing the message, meeting new people, sharing the* stories, getting people excited about their lives and the potential of their lives, what their lives could be." The extreme nature of this commitment was important to Jeff, and he felt that others would get excited about the trip if they saw others taking it seriously. His sense of extreme commitment is something that many Millennials share—and rightly has its place at times. Jeff shows a strong sense of prudence in this present life by realizing when extremes have gone too far and need to be tempered.

"I think I'm less dogmatic than I used to be. When I was in college and was reading a lot of Dan Berrigan and Dorothy Day, I was much more willing to tell people that they weren't Catholic than I am now. I think I just calmed down. I learned to listen better. I can remember telling people from Compass that they weren't Catholic because they weren't serving the poor and that Jesus said all these things about serving the poor like, 'I come to bring Good News to the poor.' I told them that if they didn't have an experience of the poor, with the corporal works of mercy, then they had no business calling themselves Catholic. I was a really self-righteous person and was a smart enough person to be able to back it up. I think I scared a lot of people off, because I was kind of a self-righteous punk!"

Jeff is brilliant for a man of his age, and challenges many of his peers to think through their positions holistically before reaching rash conclusions. He has a wonderful sense for navigating ambiguity. Recently at a three-hour Good Friday service, Jeff gave a reflection on the thirteenth station of the cross: *Jesus dies.* He weaved his way through the near impossibility of God's death. He asked the hard question, *"How could Jesus die if he was God? Does God remain alive and dead at the same time?"* His comfort with the ambiguous nature of faith was inspiring, and he offered no easy answers but clearly rested easy with a complex faith.

At the same time, Jeff has a remarkable sense of freedom. *"I guess my most profound spiritual longing is for freedom. I want to live like a jazz singer sings: with every decision a conscious choice made readily and wisely in the creation of art. I don't live like that, but I feel like people in the church help show me how. For me, what's most important about the church are not its rules—these are important, but only as a means to the end. It's the community I love—both those here and the saints in heaven—and the sacraments that bond us all. These people and events inspire me, bring me closer to God, and make me a more loving person. I want to love as well as I can, and the only way for me to do that is to be free. When it is at its best, the church gives me that freedom."*

Jeff has been involved in many social-action programs on both a national and local level and sees his call to serve the least of God's people. At times, he may even become the typically rigid Millennial Catholic in this regard, where he mulls over a decision to remain committed to teaching inner-city school-children or work more on developing his writing skills or even heading off to graduate school. He painfully struggles with his longing to love even the least among us and not to ignore those closest to him. Being Catholic for Jeff is profoundly hard. Of all those I interviewed he seemed most up to the challenge of living a faith life that was neither overly rigid nor haplessly adaptable.

"I think many of my religious experiences these days are gradual insights…over time. Whether it's on the subway, or at Mass, or with friends, or in a quiet chapel, somehow knowing that in that moment, God is real. Sometimes it's more dramatic, like if I've been away and I'm like, 'God I've been away—I'm so sorry!' But God shouldn't be a daytime talk show. Prayer doesn't have to be like that—it's a relationship. God, for me, is like someone who's already up when you've come downstairs in the morning and you're stumbling to get that cup of coffee and he's already there with his. And you sit on the front porch in a rocking chair and the sun is just starting to rise over the horizon and he says, 'It's a beautiful sunrise!' And I say, 'Yeah.' And that's it.

But I don't think it's that comfortable all the time either. God challenges us radically and has a radically different vision of the world. But at the end of the day, that vision is ultimately built on love, and what God has for us is love and presence more than anything else. How that coexists with the challenge of that vision—I don't know—but I know it does. How I understand those things I guess I'll leave to the theologians!"

I would note that knowing Jeff over this short time, there is not much that I sense he will ever leave to the theologians. His sense of what it means to be Catholic is healthy, balanced, and yet an extremely difficult challenge that places the bar a lot higher than many would dare to approach. Jeff is both daring and comforting, like a brother who chides his siblings for their failings, but who also picks them up when they fall down and skin a knee.

Dare I say, that's a whole lot like the kind of person Jesus calls us all to be.

Profile 6: Jasmin S., Twenty-six, Unit Coordinator, Catholic Charities, Builders for Family and Youth, New York City

Jasmin S. grew up on Manhattan's Lower East Side to parents who raised her in the Catholic faith. Today she has gone through a kind of role reversal. *"Over the years, because of the liberalism that has taken place in the church and the world, it seems that I'm the one who encourages them [her parents] to go to church and to keep up to date with our faith, the faith that they raised me in."*

Recently Jasmin left a corporate job in order to work for an abstinence program for teens called Builders for Family and Youth, a division of Catholic Charities, where she works as a unit coordinator for their Queens location. For her it is a return to working in the pro-life movement. She formerly worked in crisis counseling at a pro-life center in her younger days. She counseled women from the ages of twelve to forty-five who were considering having an abortion and were reaching out to the center for one last shot at not having an abortion. *"You have to have faith just to listen to all these women—one had twenty-eight abortions! You have to be strong in your faith. Prayer is the only thing that is going to get you through that experience without judging them."*

Jasmin found herself inspired by the work that the Franciscan Friars of the Renewal and the Sisters of Life were doing in the pro-life movement, and even did a "Come and See" weekend (a type of vocation discernment retreat) with the Sisters of Life. It was their inspiration that continued to solidify her commitment to pro-life causes. She gets upset easily when the commitment to pro-life causes is lacking at the parish level.

"In my parish I've had an issue with the fact that they aren't as involved in the whole pro-life movement as much as they should be. They aren't as outspoken as they should be about this! They paint everything really pretty, and the reality is that it isn't very pretty. The tragedy of abortion needs to be spoken about, and the parents of the youth in the church need to hear about this topic. At times, in order to avoid controversy they stay away from that. I've had that conversation with my pastor and other priests."

When asked how pastors should bring up this topic, Jasmin doesn't hesitate: *"It needs to be brought up in the homily and during the announcements at Mass. The groups within the church, especially the youth group, need to discuss this so that parents are aware of what's going on. I think they just don't know what's going on out there and what their kids are doing and how they handle a situation if it arises. The issues that surround abortion also need to be discussed openly in churches. Issues on sexuality and drugs and even cutting class are issues that teens experience, and parents need to know how they should handle it when issues arise."*

Jasmin's approach tends toward educating teens, but it is also obvious that she has seen a number of young adult parents who could use a class or a speaker's series on the issues surrounding abortion. *"If I were pastor I'd bring in an expert about abortion and abstinence and how to speak to your teenager about this and the importance of saving yourself [for marriage]. I'd bring in an expert on teen pregnancy because that situation is different, and we have to ask ourselves, 'What are we going to offer this child who is now pregnant?'. We need to speak about drug use and peer pressure and do role-play exercises so teens and parents have some idea on how to handle these issues should they get caught up in something."* She also recommends inviting the experts to speak to the teens and the adults separately and then reunite the groups to share what they've learned.

Jasmin's experience in the pregnancy crisis center placed her in a precarious position where she had to think on her feet and not be judgmental of the women who were seeking her assistance. Often, those who criticize the pro-life movement point to certain people within the movement who often, as I say, "steal the headlines" from those like Jasmin, who are doing the often hidden work behind the scenes in pregnancy crisis centers nationwide. The issue that I often see is that pregnancy crisis centers are not well known to the general public. Catholics in general do not know what goes on there and don't realize all the services that they provide. Jasmin agrees.

"Pregnancy care centers have plenty of organizations to refer pregnant mothers to along with parenting classes, and they even provide the mother with a crib for when the baby is born. There is help available. The Sisters of Life and the Franciscan Friars of the Renewal also have homes for pregnant mothers. So that's a great help. Within the parishes I wonder if

these things can be promoted more in the bulletins with the addresses and phone numbers of the organizations. I never see them. The Sisters of Life also send out huge packets to all the parishes about retreats for women suffering from postabortion syndrome, but either these packets don't get opened or they sit on some pastor's desk instead of getting put in the bulletin because I don't often see them."

How did Jasmin become so committed to the cause in the first place?

Her faith story takes a prominent turn in her adolescence, when she rebelled and left the church. *"I just wanted to do my own thing. I had questions and I was searching, and at one point I knew I needed something greater in my life; I just didn't know what I was missing. I finally came to terms and realized that it was God. So I started to visit different kinds of churches. My mom was upset and told me that 'I wasn't leaving the Catholic Church,' but I just kept searching, and when I was seventeen, I ended up on my first retreat at the Catholic Charismatic Center in the South Bronx.*

"The individuals in the charismatic renewal believe that they have been 'filled' or 'baptized' with the Holy Spirit, often through the laying on of hands. The signs of the 'baptism' or 'filling' may include joy, the gifts of speaking in tongues, or glosso-lalia, a slaying in the Spirit [when a person loses all motor control over their body and falls to the floor or ground, often brought on when the preacher or designated assistant comes directly to a person and lays hands on them or speaks a prayer over them]. People within the movement often feel like they now have a deeper personal knowledge of Jesus in his church and tend to make huge commitments to the church because of that. They also are very devoted to the pope, the Blessed Mother, Mass attendance, the rosary, and the way of the cross."[2]

On the retreat that Jasmin attended with a cousin, she claims that *"it was a life-changing experience. I had been raised in the church but I really didn't understand it. I was just forced to go, but at this point in my life the presence of the Holy Spirit was made a reality to me, especially understanding the role of Mary and the Eucharist...all this, in just a matter of three days, became a reality for me."*

The retreat she attended was a heavily emotional experiential weekend that is typical in the charismatic movement. Many teen communities and especially Hispanic communities have relished these experiences, with many regarding them as moments of reconversion. They engage people in a community where they feel loved and supported in a church setting. While the retreat is often led by peers, expert speakers and clergy also lead portions of the weekend.

Jasmin's retreat consisted of a simple praise and worship prayer service on Friday evening, and then *"the real work of retreat began on Saturday. An expert gave a presentation on Mary and another on the Eucharist and the importance of adoration and confession. I was like, 'Oh wow! That's why we go to confession!', and they encouraged all of us to go to confession. It was my first time in ten years."* Jasmin practically gushes over the experience when retelling the story. She was clearly and genuinely touched by the experience of this spirit-filled retreat, and it became a hallmark in her faith experience. One particular point of the retreat remains very special for her.

"On Saturday night they blindfolded you and walked you to a corner where you're alone and you're just praying. It goes on for a good hour, and it's just you and God. Toward the end of the ritual they take you by the hand and they hand you a candle and remove the blindfold and they say 'receive the light of Jesus,' and you're then standing in front of the Blessed Sacrament. After that you're basically in adoration for the next hour." It was clearly a powerful moment when the leaders provided her with two very important hallmarks of young adult life, contemplation and a strong sense of mystery and awe. The use of the blindfold gave

Jasmin a chance to block out all distractions, so that, as she says, it was just "her and God." And the Eucharist is often cited by the Magisterium of the church as being the faith's "source and summit." So what better way to reintroduce Jasmin back into "real life" than by placing her in front of the Blessed Sacrament when that blindfold was removed? It's no surprise that Jasmin is very centered in her dedication to the Eucharist.

Hispanic young adults often cite the experience of emotive prayer as being significant in their spirituality. The pentecostal churches are finding an easy time in gaining Hispanic converts to their churches by providing these emotive experiences of ritual and prayer that quite often Hispanics are hard-pressed to find in the Roman Catholic Church. The charismatic movement is often the place where many find a place in the church that speaks to their religious sensibilities.

Why is the emotion so important? Culturally, Hispanic young adults have a love for these emotional prayer experiences that we do not find, in general, among Anglo young adults. However, we need to be careful in not characterizing Hispanics as "the emotional ones," and lump their emotional experiences together into a type of anti-intellectual category. This is surely not the case, nor will the emotional prayer experiences of a retreat engender long-lasting effects. Young adult ministers need not only to provide great immediate experiences of emotion in prayer rituals and retreat gatherings, but also to follow up with a strong sense of intellectual rigor about the teachings of the church. We need to get beyond the elements of sheer emotion and sensuality and enrich that emotional experience with one that is intellectually sound and allows the young adult to have ownership of not merely an emotional moment, but a time of growing deeper in the faith tradition that they have become enraptured with. When the strings of the heart are pulled by the realization of the great love that God has for us, it is time for ministers to meet their responsibility to go further with people and promptly provide an examination of the wisdom of Catholic tradition as soon as possible to set alongside their emotional experience.

An example where this is done well is on the Charis Retreat Weekends that I run in New York. We provide many moments for young adults to share their faith struggles, through individual witness talks and small-group discussion and silent reflection. We also provide high energy liturgy, prayer services, and meditation hours throughout the weekend. In short, this is indeed an intense weekend, wrapped within a lot of emotional issues that young adults are examining. At two points during the weekend, we allow some of the intellectual agenda to take center stage by providing an opportunity for those on the retreat to ask questions of our staff. We do this by letting people write anonymous questions on index cards and place them into a box, then we later pull them out and answer them. We encourage comments and argumentative discussion, but we always provide the wisdom of the tradition from the catechism or other church documents.

While Jasmin was in her teens when she attended this retreat, young adults point to similar emotional experiences on retreat in ritual moments. The reenactment of the washing of the feet, which Charis Ministries re-creates on their retreat, is a prime example. At times, these moments are criticized by young adults as being forced or contrived moments, but for most, the moments can be lasting experiences that reveal much about their religious sensibilities and their longings for something tangible to believe in. God often is so far removed from young adult life that they long for opportunities where they can see, feel, taste, and smell the very fervor of religion.

Being able to take those moments and then have them push that experience into action in a variety of ways is another hallmark of young adult faith. It is not enough for young adults to simply have a once-a-week religious experience; rather they long to express (literally "push out") their faith into the very world they live in beyond the church doors. For Jasmin, besides her experience working for pro-life causes, a mission trip to Nicaragua gave her another opportunity to experience faith at a deeper and more tangible level. I met Jasmin on this mission trip to an orphanage for abandoned children or children with special needs. The group's mission was twofold: to provide repairs to the structure where the children are living and to help care for the needs of the children, who most often, simply want to be loved. Living in an orphanage is a tough life, with lots of neglect present, despite the best intentions of its staff. Jasmin reports, *"Being able to share with these children and experience the conditions that they live in…I can't even express it…the smiles they have on their faces daily, and you can't even imagine how they could be so happy in the midst of such poverty and handicaps. It makes you realize how much you have. I have to be smiling and be thankful to God because…I mean, look at these children! They're abandoned! They go through so much, and yet they remain with smiles on their faces. They taught me a lot about myself and the changes I had to make. I needed to examine how I spent my money. Instead of spending seven dollars on a taxi, I can send it over there so they can eat. I don't need to go out to dinner. I can go home and eat so I can donate the rest to those who do not have. When I came back here, I was changed for a short time, and then I grew back into society and 'the way it is,' so that's something I struggle with."*

These moments for Jasmin have engendered a routine of prayer in her everyday life. *"I pray daily in the morning if I'm not running late. I do meditation prayer and open my Bible randomly and meditate on the words, whatever they are. I use some pro-life newsletters and study guides with it. Also, Mass is very important. I used to go everyday during my lunch hour but now I don't have a flexible schedule. And when I pray, or go to Mass, I prefer*

*it to be in Spanish. I know that it's because that conversion expe-
rience I had was at the Hispanic Catholic Charismatic Renewal
Center, where everything took place in Spanish, and so when I'm
praying it's in Spanish, but English Mass is just as powerful."*

In short, Jasmin is not what many would define as a typical
conservative young adult, rather she is what Bacik/Reese would
define as an evangelical young adult who has been moved by her
experiences and has vigor to her convictions. Careful not to
judge, Jasmin's spirituality is not haughty or condescending.
Rather, it is a faith that expresses her longing for God to be present, even in the midst of tragedy. How can God most show himself to the world when it makes the least sense? When she sees
children who are handicapped for no good reason, Jasmin is able
to find God in them. To a woman asking for help when she is
scared and pregnant, Jasmin is the very face of God, caring and
loving that woman when perhaps nobody else can bring themselves to do so. Jasmin is also funny and down to earth in most
matters. She plays a fierce game of cards (as I know all too well
when she beat the pants off me in Nicaragua), laughs easily, and
is not stuffy or rude in her relationships with others. Her passion
for her church is what drives her. Dare I say, without the church,
I think Jasmin indeed may have become a different person.

Conclusion

The one consistency in nearly all these interviews is that
each of the young adults favors a more collaborative dialogue
between the church and young adults. They notice the lines that
people have drawn between conservatism and liberalism, but
they seem willing to try to steer past them toward something less
judgmental as a whole. Perhaps this is a huge opportunity for the
Gen X and Millennial cultures. I sense that they will be able to
do what the Baby Boomers could not accomplish—simply to

have a dialogue with one another in the spirit of unity in diversity. Cardinal Bernadin's Common Ground Initiative did not completely succeed. Maybe it took place at the wrong time and place. Young adults today need and want to have those theological conversations that explain to them the wisdom and richness of the Catholic faith. Meanwhile they have little time for rules and regulations the likes of which Dan especially met with firsthand. In the next chapters I will discuss how more collaborative dialogue can take place facilitated by young adult ministry leaders.

There are some marked differences however; Millennial young adults as a whole do have more of a longing for security and certitude than do their Gen X counterparts. By the same token, Gen Xers are spiritually enriched by being together in communal experiences but have little need for a personal or private spirituality. Both have an overwhelming need to intellectualize their faith—how does all of this make sense in the everyday? Faith for young adults is not a spectator sport. They long to integrate it into every fiber of their lives and live that faith unapologetically. When they can't do that, they mold some appropriate portions of their faith into preferential options—favoring certain aspects of faith over the whole, while many others chuck their religious connection into the trash heap in favor of a more individualistic spirituality. Still, good news is here. Of the twelve interviewees, only one (Dan) has virtually no connection to Catholicism, and even he would prefer to have a connection. When we are able to engage young adtuls, we tend to keep them in our midst. So the question we need to discuss for the remainder of this book is clear: How do we keep young adults engaged?

PART III
Ministering to Two Generations

CHAPTER 5

POPE AS ROCK STAR

World Youth Day

While research indicates that young adults often did not share the same opinions as Pope John Paul II with regard to doctrinal matters, sexuality, and even social justice, he was still regarded as someone for whom young adults had a profound respect and admiration. Why is this so? John Paul II provided the church with a valuable lesson in the staging and execution of World Youth Day.

World Youth Day is a jamboree-like event that is essentially more like World Youth Week. Hundreds of thousands of young pilgrims gather at a designated site and await the arrival of the pope, who celebrates both an evening prayer service and Mass the following morning after the young people have camped out overnight. Essentially this event may be described as "Pope as Rock Star." As John Paul II often stated, its purpose was to engage the young people in dialogue with the pope. He claimed that young people would show up by the thousands if the pope simply showed up for a day to be in their presence. His perception was quite accurate as evidenced by the large crowds that attended Denver (1993), Manila (1995), Paris (1997), Rome (2000), Toronto (2002), and Cologne (2005).

An important and clear distinction needs to be made and kept in mind. In U.S. church circles and understanding, the word *youth* is used primarily in reference and definition as those in their teenage years. In other countries *youth* has a broader-ranging definition, encapsulating those who have reached the age of consent (usually fourteen) until the age of marriage. Therefore, the word *youth* (or *jovenes,* in Hispanic culture, for instance) conveys different meanings and understandings throughout the world. Generally speaking, the "youth" that the Vatican encourages and promotes to attend this event range from the ages of sixteen to thirty-five years old.

Most American attendees of World Youth Day are often teenagers. The reasons may be described in a threefold manner: First, as stated, Americans have a tendency to simply define youth as teens. There is also confusion between the church's definition of "youth" as it differs from "young adults," and the fact that popular culture uses these terms interchangeably to describe teenagers. Second, young adults in their twenties and thirties tend not to have an entire week to spare from their work and other time-sensitive obligations. Third, the expense of attending World Youth Day often adds to the pressure of the economic strain on those in their early career lives. While quite affordable, this will be the only opportunity for many young adults for a yearly vacation. They are forced to choose between one day with the pope (and probably a slim chance of actually seeing him up close while being surrounded and cramped by thousands of others) and a more relaxing vacation spot where they can firmly recharge their batteries. The pressure of a non-stop work life often forces them to choose the latter.

I attended World Youth Day 2002 in Toronto and found this to be quite accurate. Most of the Americans I encountered throughout the week were teenagers, while several international attendees spanned ages well into their late twenties. Later in the week, I noticed quite a few more American young adults who had made their way from nearby environs to attend the pope's

Saturday evening service and possibly Sunday Mass if they could find an inexpensive place to stay. As is the case in many parishes, these young adults, while being attracted to the event, often find that most American participants there are younger than themselves or are the parents of the teens who are the overwhelming majority. Many that I know who have attended often take a "been there, done that" type of attitude toward the event, not penciling in a second trip. In short, World Youth Day for Americans is primarily an event aimed at teens.

Paul J., director of YAM in the Joliet Diocese, confirms this as a definite issue at World Youth Day. Paul, a three-time traveler to World Youth Day, admits not even realizing that World Youth Day was aimed at a non-teenage demographic.

"I was under the impression that this was an event for teenagers when I was a teen and attended World Youth Day in Denver. It wasn't until I went to Toronto (Paul led a teen ministry on the trip) nearly ten years later that I discovered a significant amount of young adults, albeit from non-English-speaking countries mostly, attending World Youth Day. I realized then that maybe I needed to ask myself how the pope speaks to me as a young adult. It's somewhat disconcerting that there weren't many young adults from North America. It was hard for me to get into the experience because for the predominant group from that part of the world it was an adolescent experience."

However, that is not to say that the event itself is a failure by any means. For teenagers who have attended these events and are now young adults we see a clear connection with Catholicity and with respect for the pope. Many of those who attended as teenagers do indeed return and furthermore help promote the event in local parishes.

One of these young adults is Jasmin S., a twenty-six-year-old Hispanic woman from Manhattan's Lower East Side. Jasmin (the subject of profile 6 in chapter 4), who first went to see the

Holy Father in Rome at World Youth Day 2000, epitomizes its sweeping success:

"I was simply trying to plan a vacation and nothing was working out, so my youth group had one spot available and I grabbed it. After the trip, I realized that it was God's plan for me to be there and not to go on a simple vacation."

Paul J. also concurs with his point that his experience as a teen at Denver's World Youth Day was a hallmark for him as a Catholic. *"I was a teenager, a junior in high school, and it was one of the first experiences I ever had with the universal church, which was kind of intimidating for me growing up in small-town Indiana. Just to see the diversity of cultures there was huge! It was something about the church that I had never really understood or appreciated before, so I guess as a teenager that really shocked and overwhelmed me, but at the same time captivated me. While being a crowded experience, it was a strange kind of crowd, not like a mall or a stadium. They were pumped and excited but in a very 'clean' way [laughs]. There was 'niceness' to it all. There was no pressure or negativity or anger. It was a giant party where there was no pressure."*

Jasmin and Paul both point out that the personality of John Paul II was the driving force behind World Youth Day for them and that through this event he was able to highlight three hallmarks of young adult life and capitalize on them. The first is simply an experience of the papacy. John Paul II's legacy will almost certainly be these World Youth Day celebrations because, unlike any other pope, John Paul was able to give the youth of the world "an experience of the pope." As Mary Jansen, the director of Campus and Young Adult Ministry in San Francisco, stated, *"For me, World Youth Day is so special because the pope took time for me. Young adults and youth were special enough to him that he intentionally took time and was present for them. That's something I'll always be thankful for and an experience I'll never forget."*

Paul concurs. *"I don't remember much about the content provided to me. To be honest, you'd have to tell me what happened there because I don't know that I remember all that. But I do remember the pope very vividly. And the pope's words too. It felt like an intimate interaction between the pope and myself. Everyone there would've said, 'Yep, he was talking right to me.' John Paul II had a way of silencing the crowds, just in the way that he spoke; you didn't want to hear anything else. You just craved to hear him speak. Now I grew up in a Polish household with my Polish grandparents and great-grandparents, so his Polish-English accent resonated with me on a deeper level, along with that innate charm that he had. When he spoke he was an older man, but he had a vibrancy that I don't think I've ever seen in somebody of his age. I can remember him stamping his feet when he wanted to make a point and waving his hand in the air...a very vibrant and expressive way of speaking that just captivated you."*

The specific words of John Paul II have stayed with Paul all these years. *"He said something during his first speech to the crowds, which was, 'Go proclaim the gospel on the housetops; don't let anyone stop you.' He was using the vernacular English that we were used to. It wasn't something antiquated or anything like that; it was real language that he was using, and so that really stuck with me."*

Even in Toronto, while Paul experienced the pope as a young adult when the pope was a much older man, he notes similarities to his Denver experience. *"The pope was different, but he still had that vibrant, playful way about him, even though he was very sick and he couldn't stamp his feet anymore. Well, he couldn't stand up anymore at that point, but his voice seemed even more determined now. When his actions couldn't do it, he used his voice to do it. But his English was slurred and he spoke*

in French as well, so while it was more difficult, there was still
something that gave me a rush of energy when he came by in
the motorcade. He still had this kind of charisma around him
that still got you."

So, first and foremost, the idea of a pope being present to young people, being visible to them, being able to look into their eyes and for him to look into theirs is a foundational achievement for which he should be given much credit. Nobody else dared to pull off an event like this, and often people tried to talk the pope out of it. John Paul II understood the value of experience, and he wanted to build an experience that young people would not forget.

A story that I often like to tell of my own World Youth Day experience begins with a conversation between one of my colleagues in ministry and me in Toronto's Exhibition Hall. We began to hear screaming at one point, and I asked what people were screaming about. The papal motorcade had begun to make its way down the street for the pope's midweek appearance, well before any of his other public World Youth Day events were held. My colleague had been to World Youth Day many times and encouraged me to walk outside to try to get a close-up glimpse of the pope. I was skeptical, thinking I would not be able to get close at all. Also, I hate crowds, and after a long career in radio, getting a glimpse of a celebrity held little novelty for me. My colleague persisted, however, and after walking outside, I was somehow able to jostle myself close to the barrier that the motorcade would pass. The next few moments are as clear to me today as they were then. The green-colored "popemobile" encased with its bulletproof glass held the pontiff somewhat slumped in his chair, and yet he was able to smile and wave slightly to the crowd. He passed right in front of me, and for a few fleeting seconds I indeed felt special. I even took out my cell phone to call my wife and my mother. Indeed, the pope has provided me, personally, with the experience of simply being in the presence of both holiness and a man who cared for those whom he knew the church would come to depend on in the not-so-distant future.

Since the experience of the papacy came to the fore with John Paul II, his successor, Benedict XVI, has a hard act to follow. Paul reports that his experience at the most recent World Youth Day in Cologne lacked some of the flair and panache that John Paul II gave to the event. *"I took a group of young adults to Cologne simply because I had noticed that many of the young adults I encountered in Toronto where not from English-speaking countries, but from Africa and Asia mostly. It was then I realized that I needed to ask myself how the pope is speaking to me now as a young adult. I had a great experience with the group I was with because they were my peers as opposed to the teenagers I led on a trip to Toronto. However, the larger experience of World Youth Day was a big disappointment. Pope Benedict wasn't really as charismatic or enthusiastic. It seemed like he was going through the motions that John Paul II had established; he was just fulfilling his obligations. That's kind of what I felt. I didn't feel the passion in Benedict's words. Did he say good things? Certainly. But did he say them with conviction and excitement? Did he say them with charisma and did he say them with attention-grabbing words? No, no he didn't. I was a little disappointed because when he passed by I didn't feel that there was anything special about it."* So it seems that John Paul II is indeed a tough act to follow.

Second, it was not merely an experience of the pope that people treasured but an experience of culture. Here, gathered in one place, were a multitude of cultures under the umbrella of Catholicism. There was no rioting; groups intermingled with one another, translators earned their paychecks, and everyone reached out to one another in an atmosphere of peace and tranquility. It is amazing to many that there weren't more problems. My boss at the time, Father Brett Hoover, remarked in Toronto that for him, *"The beauty of World Youth Day is that we've gathered all these young people from so many different cultures and places, and yet they all come together and spend time with one another, learning about their ways of life and sharing a common faith."*

Both Paul and Jasmin agreed. A highlight for both of them was that they met people from all over the world who were simply there because they were Catholic. Jasmin noted, *"Just to see the diversity of cultures there was huge. It was crowded, but it was a strange kind of crowd that was pumped and excited. They were energetic, and it was just one giant party. That's what I most remember."*

Jasmin's experience also ran counter to her usual experience of partylike atmospheres, but suggests that the aspect of the merging of cultures was certainly key. She said, *"We met people from all over the world who were singing and dancing for the Lord in their own languages, and we just walked around and got to meet these people. On that Sunday, when the pope arrived, the silence that was there, I mean, there were literally a million people there, but you could have heard a pin drop. It was total silence and total peace and the presence of the Lord was so strong. It was simply amazing."*

Finally, the aspect of awe in liturgy and ritual were clearly present. Indeed, this was a time like no other for the people who attended Mass or one of the prayer services. It was hallmarked by great music, the pope preaching relevantly to the needs of the teens and young adults, and the reverence shown by many in attendance. Catholic symbols were everywhere, from the makeshift confessionals where priests heard confessions in an open field all day long to the beauty and stillness of the evening procession of the stations of the cross. Placing the pope in the center of all this was merely the icing on the cake. Perhaps here is where Benedict will, as it seems, continue the tradition or perhaps move it in a new direction. Paul notes: *"...the crowd in Cologne was a far more pious crowd than those during the John Paul II papacy. They piously, ritually reenacted their faith rather than graciously celebrating it as in the years before. Is there a place for that? Sure, but I'm not sure that World Youth Day is that place because it didn't capture me as much as before. But there were some very contemplative moments, and this really helped in prayer, but overall, the fun of the event was lost. I tended to create the fun on my own with my group."*

Benedict may indeed be playing to a more individualistic crowd. Paul negatively notes: *"In terms of creating that energy, that motivation to go out and do something good with this faith, it wasn't there. It was replaced by attitudes of piety, prayerfulness, contemplation. We talked a lot about what the truth is, but we didn't express the idea that your Catholicity enriched the world. It was a bit more exclusive than I remember before."*

So the new face of World Youth Day and a new culture in which this event will be expressed may indeed be drastically different. Benedict XVI may be able to move people in new ways and will face the problem of following the looming shadow of John Paul II and his enthusiasm.

World Youth Day Problems

While World Youth Day is indeed like no other event, it does have some major problems.

What Next?

The overwhelming criticism of World Youth Day stems from the lack of a follow-up. Thousands of youth and young adults do attend World Youth Day, but often that does not translate into the same groups becoming active members of their parishes. It often turns into "a flash in the pan" spectacle that has no long-lasting effects on parish life or church participation. Instead, it seems to breed and promote a cult of personality more for the pope himself but not perhaps for the church as a whole.

To be fair, however, this might not be an appropriate criticism of John Paul, but rather of those in parish governance. Jasmin points out that this was not her experience at all: *"When we came back we were on fire! We brought that experience to the parish. We were asked to speak about the event and show the videos of our time in both Rome and Toronto. It made sense because we also did fund-raising for the trip from our parish, so we wanted them to see what they helped us accomplish."*

By and large, the problem with the after-event of World Youth Day again falls to the problem of the parish structures not holistically continuing the connection. Pastors need to attend World Youth Day with a contingent of their parishioners and then continue to nurture that bond upon return. Certainly, the scope and grandiosity of an event like World Youth Day cannot be equaled by parishes by any means, but the aspect of being present as a pastoral authority and guide that the pope models needs to be replicated. If there is one thing to take away from the experience of World Youth Day, indeed it is that experience with youth is something for all pastors and lay ministers to honor and continue in kind.

Preaching to the Choir with a Mob Mentality

Most of the people who attend World Youth Day are already connected to a church organization and are there merely to get close to the pope and meet other like-minded Catholics from around the globe. One may argue that if a nonbeliever simply came to World Youth Day and saw the testimony that it shows to the world, that indeed he or she might find value in the experience and in Catholicism by default. This may be somewhat simplistic thinking. World Youth Day is, simply put, a "mob mentality." For the unconverted, or even for those critical of the pope or of Catholicism, attending World Youth Day may indeed momentarily provide them with softened hearts. Yet like those who are similarly unchanged, upon the return home, the lack of a follow-up to this experience keeps them unaffiliated. So while they may whoop and scream with other integrated Catholics, they may in fact have no idea why they are doing so other than the fact that they are simply "in the moment." With the passing of the moment also go the conversion possibilities.

Perhaps the following example helps to illustrate this point. A woman with whom I attended World Youth Day in Toronto has been very critical of Pope John Paul II's papacy. Yet while in Toronto, she was clearly in the pope's corner. She yelled and screamed and clapped and hung on the pope's every word. Upon her return home she was just as critical of the pope. Without the presence of like-minded folks of this moment, my friend returned to her default setting.

Teens Trump Young Adults

As previously stated, young adults are clearly in the minority of Americans who attend the week-long events and activities of World Youth Day. However, the final two days of World Youth Day (the evening prayer service and the Mass) are events where young adults become a stronger force. With that in mind, perhaps a smaller-scale event of a single day could be aimed at young adults in their twenties and thirties each year, wherein more dialogue with bishops, priests, and perhaps even the pope himself could be harvested. The challenge of engaging American young adults with the many different forces at play in their lives is one in which World Youth Day does not score high as yet. Benedict may indeed do better with young adults than John Paul II did with teens. Only time will tell.

Peak Experience Triumphs over Catechesis

Another feature of World Youth Day, in addition to the experience of the pope being with young adults, is the catechetical sessions that bishops from various places conduct to provide teaching moments for the young. Some bishops are very vibrant and tell great stories of faith that engage the young people vigorously, and others choose to lecture in a more staid and dull way. Regardless, little seems to stick with those in the congregation. Paul claimed to *"remember very little of the catechesis and the Masses that I went to. What I ended up remembering to this day is all of the unique people that I met there."*

In short, the peaks and valleys of the day are evidence of gaping holes in the programming. The experiences of culture and the pope are so overwhelming that the rest of the activities blend into the wall paint. This also promotes a sense of religiosity that is only valid when you hit those peaks. Spirituality is more than sensuality, but it is hard to sell dry catechetical sessions when the pope is the main attraction at the Catholic rock concert.

Conclusions

Regardless of the problems with World Youth Day, overall the event is one that is laudatory. Experience indeed makes a huge difference in the lives of young adults. John Paul II has given us a great example of what it means to be present to both teens and young adults. Pope Benedict may be able to add a strong sense of contemplation and religious identity to a new kind of World Youth Day experience that indeed may be more attractive to young adults than to enthusiastic teens. Overall, however, our mission (and the pope's) is not merely to depend on World Youth Day to expose young people to this kind of papal presence. The pope certainly needs to be present to young adults, but there is a need to go beyond this presence. Rather, we must take the concept of World Youth Day, integrate it into the life of our parishes, and make it available to those seeking to connect with Catholicism. How are we present to young adults? How do we celebrate our Catholic culture within a pluralistic society? How do we provide moments of contemplation for young people in a noisy world? The next few chapters will attempt to show us how to answer these questions and a whole lot more.

CHAPTER 6

WHAT ARE THEY LOOKING FOR? WHO IS IT THEY SEEK?

Understanding Ministry with Millennials and Gen X

The great theologian Karl Rahner notes that, "We are the question which rises up before us, empty, but really and inescapably, and which can never be settled and never be adequately answered by ourselves."[1]

Indeed, young adults of all kinds are on a search for answers. In a sense they are, in Rahner's own words, "infinite questioners" in life. As they come into further knowledge they simply ask more questions. New answers often lead to more questions, and what we presume as clarities almost always trail off into obscurities with further knowledge. We never have full certainty. Thus we often rely on faith to provide those unanswerable questions with a satisfactory or a certain answer.

Longings for young adults also fall into the same category. We should take notice that, unlike their parents, many young adults no longer work for the same company for thirty years and retire with a gold watch. That kind of vocational mentality no longer applies. This is a generation that might not simply change jobs, but also careers often. Like the questioning nature of young adults, the longing nature of their lives also waxes and wanes. What they thought to be their life's work one day may abruptly cease to capture their imagination any longer. The novelty of a new career ends quickly, especially with the rise of new technologies and an expanding job market.

Young adult angst often comes from this ceaseless questioning/longing because they live in a world of immediate gratification, the world of Google. Answers can be arrived at by the touch of a button or the click of a mouse. The result is a world that young adults live in where they expect answers that are simple, clear-cut, and require little thought. They expect that if you follow the rules and do everything that is expected of you, that life indeed will reward you. Vocationally, they often follow a path that leads them to follow simple steps toward getting into the right college, graduate, or professional school in hopes that their career will lead them to a satisfactory life. If this vocation crumbles or unexpected tragedies take place, so too does all in which they've put their "faith."

Knowing that there is something beyond our categorical experience, namely *transcendent experience*, is the first step in an adult faith. And it must be the first step we take in preaching the truths of our tradition to young adults. We, in fact, are more than our jobs, our wallets, or our accomplishments. We have a transcendent nature in a world that often teaches us that the opposite is true. The walls of black and white, where simple rules are followed, need to be torn down in favor of opening us to a world that may lack some clear definition at times, but surely it is a world enriched with the spirit of God. We are more than this moment we are living in, so the simplicity of immediacy can easily be made into a false God.

However, a further point to keep in mind is that young adults live in a world of unlimited choices. Black and white thinking is often used as a remedy. It cuts through the process of thinking about the myriad of choices and makes a choice unambiguous. It allows someone else, who presumably has worked out the answers for you, to provide them to you on a silver platter.

Often religious fervor leads young adults into this trap. They are given a spirituality instead of being offered one. Millennial young adults, especially, find it difficult to navigate past this world into a spirituality that challenges them to reach beyond the simplistic world of certainty. Faith indeed is never certain.

Rather, it is when we sit with the ambiguities of everyday life, realizing that God is far beyond comprehension and yet closer than our own heartbeat, it is then that we have the makings of a solid and deep spirituality.

As Catholics we believe that the drive of human knowing is always toward God. All of our thinking and knowing takes place in that context.[2] God is our lure, of which we are able to know all that we can know, and yet goes beyond our comprehensibility. Paradoxically, we transcend the finite toward the infinite and comprehend what we know in terms of what is incomprehensible.[3] Thus as young adults inevitably begin to question the world around them, they gain more knowledge about themselves and the world. As they do so, they eventually encounter angst, or longing for something more. Something is always out of grasp. The finality of this grasping is what theologians like Rahner call God. If young adults can place their lives, filled with infinite questions of meaning, in the light of this anthropology, their world suddenly makes some sense as opposed to a world in which their limited goals have led to repeated longing, sometimes resulting in meaninglessness in the here and now. Second, when a world of black and white spirituality leaves them in shallow water, young adults find the need to place critical thought at the heart of their spirituality for it to measure up.

How should we approach the different types of young adults, all the while keeping critical thought in the mix without overwhelming these young people, who have all too much information already being thrust in their direction? The answer provides both clergy and lay ministers with a wide-ranging approach to ministry that serves the needs of young adults of this generation very well. I use the term *minister* here to describe both the clergy and the laity who work with young adults in ministry.

Hallmark 1: "Be in the World"

Ministers need to be intentionally engaged in the world in which young adults live and, at the same time, need to encourage a frequent escape or retreat from that world in order for them to reflect and offer criticism about it. After all, we can only know people by taking them where they are in their world of experience. At the same time, that does not mean that we simply take people where they are and leave them there. We must encourage a spiritual search that takes people into transcendence, a going beyond oneself and one's categorical world. As Rahner states, "The experience in which we become conscious of ourselves is one of radical questioning. We question various causes and explanations offered by the limited anthropologies of which we are aware."[4] It is only through radical questioning that young adults can come nearer to self-discovery and, in turn, closer to the divine mystery. Therefore, we need to encourage young people to question their experiences in the world in the light of faith. What spiritual tools can we give them for discernment? How much time can we offer them? How well do we really understand them? Do we take time to mentor them properly and not simply toss them the catechism and send them on their way? Do we engage their questions in both our homilies and reflections well? Are we speaking to their experience or are we otherworldly, placing ourselves on a respectable pedestal to be admired but never challenged?

This does not mean, however, that we need to be consumed by their world. Too often we run into the other extreme, where we talk in young adult language but fail to convey religious imagery as well. A priest recently told me that he tried to throw young adult terms like "iPod Nano" into his homily, even when they did not relate to what he was talking about. While he garnered a strong reaction on the cool meter, I doubt that the young people he preached to ever really heard more than the reference.

A better suggestion for ministers is twofold:

a. Use the technological world to deliver the message, but not merely be the message.
b. To take a page from Father John Cusick, the director of young adult ministry in Chicago: "Explain lots, assume little," especially when using religious language and imagery.

Why You Must Be Using Technology

We cannot afford to *not* be immersed in technology as a church. A first point of reference is that Google has become the first place people search for *anything*. So when a young adult, fresh out of college, moves to Chicago for a new job, they are more likely to search on Google for "Roman Catholic Churches in Chicago" than they would be to pick up the phone to call 411 for information or look in a phone book (or even to walk down the street to find a church in their neighborhood).

Second, we need to use the technological world to simply allow others to hear and read our messages. We need to construct Web sites, blogs, podcasts, and vodcasts (more on all of these later) to transmit our messages in several new ways, as opposed to merely assuming that young people will grasp them from the pulpit.

The second minihallmark here is to be sure that we are not creating a navel-gazing spirituality that speaks of and uses modern culture but does nothing to transcend it. As Isaac Hecker, the founder of the Paulists, once said, "…we need to profess old truths in new forms." In Hecker's case he was speaking of the construction of the printing press. Today the Paulists continue the publishing apostolate, Paulist Press, and are also engaged in making movies, Web sites, podcasts, blogs, and a whole lot more.

As we profess these truths however, we cannot simply assume that young people will have the slightest idea about the deep richness of our tradition. For some they may be hearing these things for the first time. (And for many, it may be the first time they have heard these truths professed well and with depth!) Symbols and rituals may indeed be foreign to them—very other-worldly—if you will. In helping develop their sense of transcendence we need to help them build a vocabulary and a familiarity with ritual and Catholic expression. So we need to explain lots when we are engaged in these and assume little without being condescending or unchallenging (chapters 7 and 8 will address these concerns).

Hallmark 2: Sensitively Invite the Eclipsed

Dean Hoge and his colleagues pointed out in their recent sociological study that the one thing that most Catholics find fundamental to the faith is a belief that we must serve the needs of the poor and needy. Young adults, often at the forefront of many altruistic endeavors, often also find a way to express their spirituality in this context.[5]

With that in mind, we can obviously use our commitment to social justice to engage people who are outside the doors of the church. Often this is a point of entry for young adults outside the church. In my own parish, we have found that many people who are not regular churchgoers started their engagement with us through one of our many social justice ministries, like our homeless shelter, our mission trip to Nicaragua, and our banquet for the hungry. It is usually when they experience these justice-based ministries in action that they gain a respect for the parishioners and clergy who are also taking part, and seek to inquire further into the parish's other offerings. Parishes often make intentional efforts during or after the services provided to the needy that help to merge Catholic social teaching with these programs. This helps to make the local and the global church interchangeable in the minds of those who experience it. These acts now become not merely "nice things to do" but rather "things we must do because we are Catholics."

This is much like what Karl Rahner would call a ministry to the "anonymous Christians." Rahner's ground-breaking theory of the anonymous Christian states that "instead of regarding non-Christian religions, and even atheistic humanism, in a totally negative fashion, the Christian can truly learn from them, since the grace of God in Christ is or can be operative in these traditions, as it is in the hearts of all men and women."[6] Simply put, Rahner believed that if we see someone doing Christlike things in the world, that betrays the fact that Christ is indeed working in them, although they may not even be aware of his presence. They are anonymous Christians. Therefore, Rahner would have great regard for the eclipsed. While religion (or even Christ) may not exist in the forefront of their minds, they are still part of our grace-filled world and thus may indeed be living lives of great spiritual significance as anonymous Catholics in a secular world. We can opportune these Christlike acts into conversion moments.

Second, the invitation itself in liturgical ministries needs to be extended much more than it has been in the recent past. We need to invite the gifts and talents of young people to be at the heart of our parish's life. Simply put, people enjoy doing things that they do well. How well do we understand our parish? Can we identify people's gifts and talents easily? Do we even make an effort to get to know people well enough so that we can regard their gifts as holy? I know of a man with a PhD in economics who has never been asked by his pastor to be on the finance council, even though he has mentioned his desire to do so several times.

Hallmark 3: Respect the Private

Those who prefer to engage in private prayer range from those who sit in the corner of a church during Mass to those who simply have no use for church ritual at all, preferring to worship in solitary. For those in the latter camp, in the seventh volume of his *Theological Investigations* Karl Rahner makes a case for preserving the old rituals while being open to change at the same time. For Rahner there is room for both: "…in the future the preservation of our spiritual heritage is important. But it is not the ultimate and definitive factor. For it is possible to preserve a heritage only if one keeps abreast of what is new and what belongs to the future. Mere conservatism is sterile and cannot of itself attain its legitimate goals."[7]

Some private young adults prefer their way of praying and contemplating the divine to the ways of tradition. So we find both openness and a criticism of the church here. As church we must be like Rahner, who has no trouble in accepting the need and even the preference for a private spirituality. Yet we continue to hold great regard for the communal life and the tradition of praying together at Mass. It is only within the community where we can truly find faith because we are social creatures by design. Rahner writes: "The community of those who have been called out of the world, all of whom are in Jesus Christ, the Body of Christ, the house of God which the Lord has built—this community, therefore, is a reality, and can be so which has, at least in a certain sense, a *priority* over the individual, so that it sustains him and without it he himself would not be what in fact he is, and could not act as in fact he is able to act as a member of such a community" (author's emphasis noted).[8] We become different people when we interact in community. We are moved by others' generosity, love, and even hate. We react to things in society both positively and negatively. We are concerned for the needs of the least of us out of our common humanity. We would not be any of these things if we locked ourselves in a closet and simply stayed there.

It is a healthy balance between the private and the communal that we all should adopt and encourage among young adults. But how? Here are several ideas on how to merge the two:

Adoration of the Blessed Sacrament

Adoration groups enable young people to maintain their personal piety while being in the community. Some groups meet together for an hour or so of adoration mixed with both good music and moments of contemplative silence. Some take turns throughout the course of the day or week and then come together in communal prayer at the end of the weeklong or day-long ritual. Some end with a retreat experience or a day of reflection after the individual weeklong experience. The adoration of Jesus in the Blessed Sacrament is a highly personal experience and often a private one that places the central element of our Catholic faith face to face with young adult experience. However, we need to guard against the individualism that much of today's modern lifestyle often encourages. We need both the vertical aspects of relating to God (relationship between me and God; personal relationship with Jesus) alongside the horizontal aspects of the same relationship (seeing God among us, in one another, in service, etc.). Quite often those of us who have worked with Gen Xers did great work with the horizontal but lousy work with the vertical. Millennial young adults often prefer the reverse—adoration is great, but I do not need to pray or relate to anyone else but God. Ministers need to temper that with a dose of community in addition to the strong experience of private adoration. Too much of either is a serious mistake.

A strong catechesis on the Eucharist is also a must here. I have seen many communities that get dozens of young adults at adoration services but they cannot get any of them to attend Sunday Mass (and certainly not weekday Mass). We need to remind young adults that the most important experience that they can have with the Eucharist is when we come together on Sunday and break bread and eat the body of our risen Lord.

Opportunities for Meditation: (Taizé Prayer, Yoga Prayer, Centering Prayer, and the Rosary)

Chant and contemplative silence have long served the church well. Many young adults crave silence and quiet but are oftentimes afraid of it. The opportunity to experience these silent experiences in a group provides them with a good mix of community and contemplation. Taizé prayer attracts those who may like to sing and even more who simply like to listen to the meditative sounds of chant (Remember when those monks won a Grammy?).

Yoga prayer or prayer of heart and body simply uses the postures of yoga in a Christian context. Active people looking for a method of exercise coupled with meditative experience in a Catholic context may well be suited for this.

Centering prayer can be coupled with these or may be an experience all by itself. Many young adults look for a mentor to tell or show them how to pray. By giving them someone who has experience in centering prayer and allowing them to also experience it, we can provide a rich start in developing this kind of contemplative life.

The rosary meanwhile is identifiably Catholic while also being extremely meditative. The devotion to Mary that is often equated with the rosary is also attractive to young adults in heavily

Protestant areas that have anti-Catholic biases and certain cultural communities with deep devotions to Our Lady (Guadalupe celebrations among Hispanics come to mind).

Sunday Mass: Mixing Contemplation with Community Throughout

At a recent conference, Bishop Joseph Estabrook, an auxiliary bishop with the Military Archdiocese was able to exhibit exactly what I mean when I say that Mass needs to be a mix of contemplation and community. After a rousing opening hymn and a strong welcome by the bishop-presider he simply asked that the congregation hold hands. He proceeded to start the penitential rite with the following words:

"Think about a time in your life when you weren't able to reach out to someone else; when you weren't able to hold someone's hand; when you were too concerned with yourself to care for someone else. For those times, we now say...Lord Have Mercy."

There was not a single person who was offended or unmoved by that prayer. It sat in the midst of our everyday lives and bonded us strongly in the midst of one another. It also was not haughty or preachy, but rather pointed out an obvious failing that many of us probably know all too well.

For the remainder of the Mass, Bishop Estabrook mixed moments of silence at the appropriate times with the communal prayers of the Mass. His homily was engaging and merged Catholic thought with common experience. Music was both rousing and lively and stark and contemplative. Overall, it was what all of our communities should aim for with all of our rituals: a good mix of the contemplative with the community—the vertical relationship with God alongside the horizontal.

Hallmark 4: Respect Other Faiths

Rahner's theory of the anonymous Christian comes again into play here. Ecumenical dialogue and ecumenical theology have a basis that goes beyond discussion of where we can simply agree or disagree. "It is an attempt to render comprehensible to one's partner a more precisely defined expression of something that one has already grasped as his own faith and which he had laid hold of as his own truth."[9] We already possess a unity of faith at the level of God's justifying grace by virtue of our birth. So therefore our differences in faith need not be our starting point in this dialogue. We can and should start from the basis of seeing, for example, the Methodist as an anonymous Catholic and vice-versa.

In ecumenical marriage circles (where most ecumenical issues often come to light) this has proven to work well. What values and traditions do the couple share? Why would they even think about getting married to one another? What drew them to love one another? These factors often prove to be larger elements of a relationship than theological differences are. When placed in the concept of the "anonymous" on both sides, great understanding of the value of living a moral life that collectively people of all faiths enjoin is unquestionably a major revelation for the ecumenically minded and serves to build bridges among people of faith.

A young man, Matthew Lang, who was on a recent retreat with me, said it best when speaking about the relationship he has with his fiancée, a Protestant. *"How can I discount all that her faith has given to her? I fell in love with her and respect her values. Obviously her faith formed her and gave her the values I respect her for, so how can I discount her faith as an invalid one?"*

At the same time, a Catholic identity can engender a huge longing that many people hope to express. How can we respect other traditions while remaining unapologetic about our own? My thought is that our tradition has "insular rituals" that are particular to Catholicism. Mass, rosary, confession, adoration, Eucharist—all express our Catholic identity. We should offer these rituals often while not denigrating the practices of others in private. When invited to other traditions' rituals we should attend with an eye toward understanding their beliefs. How do they best express what they have come to believe and what are the commonalities with the tradition of Catholicism?

Invitation again is important in ecumenical relations. Do we hold seminars with members of other denominations in order to come to a better understanding of one another? Do we invite them to our social functions in our community? Do we point out the good works they do and offer to lend a hand in their social justice activities in the communities we serve? We need a continual invitation to other faith traditions in order to understand both our own tradition as well as those of others.

Hallmark 5: Guard against Fundamentalism but Wield Symbolism Well

Some young adults flock to praise and worship services filled with vibrant music and hold an emotive sense of prayer in high regard. "They hope to use all their senses in prayer." Father James Bacik cautioned earlier that "a few [evangelicals] are really fundamentalist, who act aggressively in preserving their Catholic heritage from the threats of the contemporary world and the reforms of Vatican II, which appear to them as excessive and dangerous."[10]

Karl Rahner cautions people to be on guard against an "unthinking piety" and a "false intellectualism." In this grouping of young adults we may see aspects of both. The emotive sense of prayer limits our aspect of transcendence and mystery, placing God only in the experience of our senses. However, it is in our senses that we experience all that we do, and therefore it is a necessary element of being human. It would justifiably be correct then to use sense as a mediator to get to transcendence. The problem that usually happens here is that many stop with the sensual feelings of the moment. The categorical replaces the transcendent in such a way that it blocks actual transcendent experience. Leaders of liturgical practice need to take great care in providing moments for reflection and quiet in liturgy as an opportunity to go beyond ourselves in transcendence. Appropriate silence and reverence during liturgy can serve us well in this regard.

Second, and most threatening to our young adult culture, is the experience of fundamentalism. We must combat a literal interpretation of scripture and note the differences between dogma (unchanging teaching) and doctrine (teaching that may change over time), with a proper rendering of the scripture and doctrine, complete with historical context and an appreciation of story and myth to guard against fundamentalism.

At the same time there is a huge difference between knowing our tradition well and being a fundamentalist Catholic. Communities with attitudes of Catholic fundamentalism polarize their members and "outside" those in disagreement with them or with aspects of Catholic tradition. Occasionally, communities even stifle those who attempt to carefully reconstruct a Catholic position by challenging what is presently found to be flawed within the tradition—even when they point to the tradition to evidence their point of view. (As an example, someone can point to voting for a pro-choice politician not because of their views on the subject of abortion but because they serve the needs of the poor—a very Catholic position. However, because of their stance on abortion, fundamentalist Catholics do not look at the rest of the docket, claiming that the issue of life supercedes all other issues.) Rahner suggests that the fundamentalist outlook is not the ideal. "We should be a community which attempts to avoid polarization and try to construct a healthy pluralism in which various groups hold strong convictions but show tolerance and charity toward other groups."[11]

The growing problem with accepting pluralism is that it often leads to the transmission of the idea that all religions are equal and therefore the distinctiveness of Catholicism gets "watered down" or even evaporates entirely. Certainly there is reason for alarm here. However, the alarmist tendency is to construct "extreme Catholicism," where believers are a type of "Catholic Taliban" (a term cited by those who form these kinds of communities — so I use the word not to titillate here), which often serves to alienate more than to construct.

In my personal research I have often found that these fundamentalist Catholics try to control and manipulate others. We cannot become "ecclesiological introverts who think only of the church [institutional] and not of the people."[12] I think often the leaders in these communities attempt to remove their followers from an everyday sense of faith based in their daily experience and place them within a limited experiential realm that locks them inside a clannish group. God indeed needs to be found in the world and not merely in church circles. Often, God gets relegated to a Sunday or church-only sense of faith. Therefore one may never grow to see faith outside of the church walls as an integral part of human experience. Instead God becomes Santa Claus: only available when I wish him to be around on Sunday, and during that time he'd better fulfill all my transcendent needs.

The goal, however, is to help official members of the church appropriate more of their Catholic faith, but this must be done not by appealing to authority but by drawing on the parishioners' fundamental Christian convictions. "There is no point in giving a person who is now in touch with the church, but has some reservations, the impression that at every moment that he is really a tolerated guest and not a full member of this believing community and society."[13] In short, young adults need to know what the church community believes, why they believe it, and then make a choice to believe it or not. That, in the simplest terms, takes time. They need mentors to help them form the meaning of what theological convictions they espouse to be true and which ones they would like more information about to discern where the wisdom of the tradition truly lies. This will serve to form deep conviction in the lives of young adults in a way that serves not to alienate, but rather to attract those who see the way the lives of the converted are changed.

Finally, we need to use symbolism well in our parishes. Most of the time, especially for new Catholics, the symbols and rituals of our religion get lost all too easily. A poor solution is to simply cut out all the symbols and rituals. One Catholic church decided to remove all the statues from their church because "half the people didn't know who they were anyway!" Another moved their midnight Mass on Christmas to ten p.m. A third moved the tabernacle to a small room out of view of the congregation.

If people do not know who the saints are, we can put signs nearby with their names on it. A little plaque with a brief story about the saint would be even better. The church that moved midnight Mass found several people at the church door at 11:50, only to be disappointed. Christmas is a huge time of evangelization for people. One of the most identifiable religious rituals in Catholicism is midnight Mass on Christmas. For those not already engaged in a parish, they will expect it and will be alienated from the parish should they show up and be disappointed. An important axiom to consider: Midnight Mass, Good Friday, Easter Sunday, Palm Sunday, and perhaps even Mother's Day are opportunities where many Catholics are brought to church by a well-meaning relative. We have an opportunity to get them to think about returning. These disengaged parishioners expect these services to be at a usual time, so moving an identifiable Mass like Christmas midnight Mass or the Easter Vigil serves no useful purpose. These Masses are generally not done for the sake of regular parishioners but rather for infrequent guests.

Finally, if the Eucharist is the source and summit of our faith as Catholics, why would we want to hide the place we keep it? This is one of the reasons that adoration is popular again—it's identifiably Catholic. Especially in the southern parts of the United States, things that are identifiably Catholic are revered. Saints, rosaries and the Eucharist are just three of the things that a group of young people that I know in Tennessee mentioned when I asked them what kind of Catholic materials they search for on the Internet. With that in mind, tabernacles should have a prominent location in the church, so they may be found, not hidden.

When you are faced with the prospect of engaging young adults, it is best to keep these principles in mind. But what of the specifics of all of this? How do we actually *do* ministry with young adults? Where do we start? How should we proceed? The next chapter will attempt to address these questions.

CHAPTER 7

DOING MINISTRY

Fifteen Initial Steps in Starting a Young Adult Ministry

This chapter will explore the specific steps recommended in starting a young adult ministry. Many of the attempts to "do ministry" included in this chapter I have tried myself, and others have been tried by colleagues with much success. I assume nothing at the onset of this chapter with regard to the particulars of your community, diocese, campus ministry, or retreat house. However, I do note that all of the steps outlined here, simply put, work well regardless of location. These come from the perspective of a young adult minister just starting out, who has been handed the task of building a ministry and has no experience in doing so. He or she has done nothing more at this juncture than just reading the first six chapters of this book. So this is basic training in ministry, if you will.

I also caution people not to merely skip around in this chapter. One step often depends on the previous step. So I suggest reading this chapter straight through, making notes with regard to your particular community as you read. I would also recommend keeping an open mind throughout this chapter. Often we all have a tendency to say at first glance: "That would never work here!" Sitting in the ambiguity of the start of building young adult ministry is painstakingly nerve wracking. Even worse, when rebuilding or adjusting your approach to ministry after lackluster attempts to build one, it is even tougher to dismiss our preconceived notions.

Lastly, my ministry motto to keep in mind:

Rome wasn't built in a day, but boy, did it fall fast!

I recommend starting out slow with each step; understand that sweeping changes are most often "flash in the pan" experiences. Only a few things may be able to be accomplished over the course of a short period of time, so enjoy little victories and note large defeats. Trying to do too much too fast only leads to disappointment.

There are fifteen steps to follow that I recommend when starting a young adult ministry:

1. Understand your audience. (If you've read the previous chapters, you've already completed this step—congratulations!)
2. Take inventory.
3. Discern the gifts of leadership and the planning of events.
4. Use technology in as many ways as possible (more on this in chapter 8).
5. Go where you think you should not be; do what you think you should not do.
6. Always be mindful of the transcendent.
7. Always provide and emphasize safe space.
8. Always be available.
9. Appreciate gifts.
10. In your case, Sunday is a workday. In their case it's their one time to connect with you.
11. Check out other churches.
12. Provide challenges.
13. Highlight the wisdom of tradition.
14. Evaluate your strengths.
15. Pray in thanksgiving and for future discernment.

Understanding Your Audience and Taking Inventory

Taking Stock of Young Adults

You have already taken stock of the generalities in young adult life if you have read the first few chapters. We can now focus on the specific needs of your community. Two Paulist priests whom I regard as mentors, Father Brett Hoover and Father Eric Andrews, took on the difficult task of constructing a young adult ministry group when I first joined my parish, St. Paul the Apostle in New York City. Their solution started with an idea to identify young adults in the parish who would be both gifted and willing to serve on a young adult steering committee. I use the term "steering committee" as opposed to "leadership board" because it sounds less committal. A young adult may not have time to commit to a board of directors, but they very well may have time to help out on a committee. Fathers Brett and Eric merely looked at the parish rolls to see who the lectors and eucharistic ministers were in the parish and how many of those people were young adults. They also visited the parish's homeless shelter and found more young adults already present there. From that list of young adults they discerned who in that group of people would be good leaders. They also were mindful of diversity and culture so that the steering committee would look like the faces present in the parish. Simply put, they took inventory: Who is already here among us that would be able to form peer leadership for young adults? The result was a ten-person steering committee: five men and five women from all walks of life and cultures. This group formed the core of St. Paul the Apostle's Young Adult Group for the next year.

This provided the group with two things. First, young adults themselves were able to offer their own gifts and have a sense of empowerment in the ministry. For those who were theo-logically educated, they were able to assist the priests in some of the religious programming. Meanwhile others were able to pro-vide more of the social or service aspects, relieving the priests and lay ministers involved of that responsibility so they could concentrate on theological matters and be a pastoral presence for people at the various events.

I recommend taking some added steps today. More than ever we need to be aware not just of cultural and gender diver-sity but the theological diversity of young adults. Now that we know the different "types" of young adults defined in our previ-ous chapters, we have the obligation of trying to get these varied individuals involved in leadership. Their different longings will allow us to have a wide-ranging ministerial approach—there will be something that appeals to everyone because your steering committee reflects not only the cultural or gender diversity of the young adult community but also their different ways of express-ing their Catholicism. So keep in mind that we need different types of programming for the different types of young adults. Some of the theological programming will require assistance from you as the coordinator or from a priest or deacon (if you are a lay minister).

Taking Stock of Ritual

Taking inventory of ritual requires a lot of honesty and a dis-missal of preconceived notions. We often think that we are doing ritual well, and we dismiss complaints about it rather easily. When we look around on Sunday and see a dearth of young adults in the pews we should start to enumerate a number of questions:

a. ENGAGEMENT: What is the Sunday Mass experience like for young adults? Do we even see many of them at

Sunday Mass? Are they engaged when they are at Mass, or are they just going through the motions? How do we reach out to people who aren't in the pews?

b. TIME: What time are Masses held? Is this a convenient time for young adults in the area?

c. WELCOMING: Are people welcomed in our church? Are they invited to share their gifts? Are young adults active as lectors or eucharistic ministers, and are they invited to do so as well?

d. MYSTERY: Do we have that sense of awe in our parish? Do we express our ritual well, or do we just go through the motions? Have we maintained both a reverent and a contemplative attitude mixed in with our sense of communal prayer and welcoming?

e. MUSIC: Is music singable? Uplifting? Contemplative? A mix of all three? Or have we resorted to music that would depress Mary Poppins? Are young adults active in singing both in the choir and in the pews?

f. MOMENTS OF RETURN: How are we doing in regard to marriage preparation? Do we offer time to bereaved young adults before or after a funeral takes place? Do we provide baptism classes and direction in child rearing for parents? Are we available to young adults when they need someone to mentor them through difficult times?

g. CONTEMPLATIVE RITUAL: What else do we offer outside of Mass? Do we leave the church open for people to come and pray during the day? Do we expose the Blessed Sacrament for adoration frequently and intentionally? How available are we for confession? Is the church quiet during the day or is there always a lot going on during the week that disturbs the opportunity for contemplation? In urban areas this is especially important.

A quick check on the parish's outreach to young adults will give you a good indication of why they are or are not in the pews.

Taking Stock of Our Community

Where are young adults outside of the walls of the church? What is offered to young adults by others, perhaps in our own neighborhood, that they find engaging? How can we invite and become more involved with young adults in the secular realm?

A word from Captain Obvious: "If they are not in your pews on Sunday, they've got to be going somewhere!"

It's your job to find out where they are going. This will provide you with many ideas on how to connect with them later on. You should also start attending some of these events yourself. I know of a local parish priest who gets himself invited to both the local community board meeting and the boards of local condos and co-op apartments simply so he can show his face and say hi. Another joined the local YMCA, so people are now working out next to "Father." A young adult minister I know formed a play group for neighborhood families in the local park (All the parents were young adults!) in order to find out what issues young families are facing. Another religious education director is simply present in the local diner that young people frequent, while another goes to a favorite nightclub from time to time. If you can simply make a friend or two at these places that may be an entry point into getting them to think about heading into the doors of your church later. When young adults experience solid ministry, the news spreads like wildfire. Suddenly new people are checking in, wondering what the buzz is about.

Taking Stock of Our Evangelization

To steal a line from Father John Cusick: "Jesus didn't put a sign on a palm tree and say, 'All those willing to be disciples, please meet here at 1:00 p.m. on Sunday; refreshments will be served.'"

Jesus *personally invited* Simon Peter, John, even Judas into his midst. He called them by name. Fathers Hoover and Andrews did the same in their parish after they discerned who from their list of young adults might be good steering committee members. I was but one of these people about twelve years ago, and that invitation changed my life. I eventually left a twelve-year career in radio behind for a ministry position after serving on my young adult steering committee as a volunteer for a number of years. So know that your invitation could have wide-ranging effects.

We need to continually invite young adults into our ministry opportunities. This is an indispensable part of ministry. Not only do the clergy and the lay ministry staff need to do the inviting, but they need to encourage and even demand that young adults involved in ministry continue to invite people to join them.

Some poor excuses for invitations:

a. PARISH BULLETINS: I know few young adults who even read their parish bulletins, or at least I doubt that few read them in depth. Regardless of a printed announcement in a parish bulletin, young adults are compelled to join events when they are directly invited by another—especially another person whom they value.

b. PARISH PULPIT ANNOUNCEMENTS: Pulpit announcements work with young adults only when they are made by young adults themselves. There is no need for a skit or a song and dance about a scheduled event, but rather a brief and simple announcement detailing the event is sufficient. Having a young adult leader announce an upcoming event simply gives it legitimacy in the eyes of other young adults. Care needs to be made in selecting someone to give the announcement, as public speaking is not everyone's gift.

c. WEB SITE ANNOUNCEMENTS: Web postings are a wonderful way to get your message out to lots of people. However, some fatal flaws exist with them. First, there is always a need to post a direct way to contact someone for more information along with the ad itself (and it should be a "one-click" e-mail address launch). Second, people should be able to register for the event or RSVP online. Again, the need for immediate gratification needs to be paid attention to. Web site announcements should never be your only means of communication, however. You always should be relishing the opportunity to speak with a young adult one on one.

d. WEB ADVERTISING: If you are fortunate enough to have some monies budgeted for advertising, using the Web can be a good opportunity. However, placing an ad on your parish's Web page or even your diocesan one might be a recipe for disaster. A better solution would be to advertise on a secular Web site that young adults actually visit on a regular basis. This unfortunately is a much more expensive solution. Second, an ad of this type needs to be edgy. BustedHalo.com had great success with a one-line text ad entitled, "How's your halo hanging? Join us for a weekend and find out!" The ad was linked to our retreat's registration page, which detailed the weekend and gave young adults the opportunity to register. Check out Web sites that young adults in your area frequent—you may be surprised to find out that some aren't as expensive to advertise on as you would have thought.

e. E-MAIL ANNOUNCEMENTS: E-newsletters (sometimes known as "e-mail blasts") are a great way to get your message in the hands of one particular person at a time. You are directly getting a message to him by publishing an e-mail newsletter or a "blast" (a simple weekly e-mail filled with upcoming announcements). We use a wonderful service at BustedHalo.com called Vertical Response (www.verticalresponse.com), and colleagues of mine speak volumes about Constant Contact (www.constantcontact.com). Check out both of these userfriendly programs. E-mails should be sent out as infrequently as possible. Being associated with spam mail (junk e-mail) is not a good thing and will cause you to be ignored not by a few young adults but by many. Your e-mail will always be very easy to ignore. So a once-a-week e-mail announcement is a good measure for a frequently mailed young adult events listing or a magazine.

With this in mind, you want to always be gathering e-mail addresses for your list. And the way to do that is to personally invite people to sign up for your list. When you speak at a conference, sign people up for e-mail. Have a list handy in the back of church so when a young adult approaches you, the invitation to stay connected is also handy. The personal touch never goes away. In fact, it's your first connection. E-mail simply keeps people more easily connected—but it almost never establishes a strong *initial* connection with anyone.

A final word of caution: never sell your e-mail list to anyone. EVER.

Whenever you are contacted by e-mail, you should take extra care to make sure that the person feels invited and welcomed to your events and your ministry group in general.

Here is an example of the opening paragraph of a retreat e-mail that I send out when someone writes to me requesting information about the retreat program we run out of my ministry in New York:

Hi there,

    My name is Mike Hayes and I'm one of the directors for the Charis Retreat that you recently inquired about. Know that we are very much looking forward to having you join us.

    [Description of retreat program in brief]

    [Next steps to register in brief along with a direct link to register online]

    There are several clergy and lay ministry directors who will also be available for individual consultations (pastoral counseling) if you wish to explore a particular issue you may facing in depth, throughout the weekend as well. Know that our staff is here for you should you require someone to talk to outside of the peer sessions we offer.

    In short, many people have really enjoyed the retreats, and they have returned for another visit with us. We hope you can join us and we really welcome your presence on the weekend.

    If you have any questions please don't hesitate to e-mail or call me: mike@bustedhalo.com or 212 265 3209 x205.

Thanks,

Mike Hayes

    In the above example, we have extended a huge welcome, described the program, made it easy for them to register, provided a source to write or call for more information, given them counseling information if they would like it, and thanked them a final time. I cannot tell you the number of responses I get from people who report that this simple e-mail upon request convinces them that the retreat is worth their time.

Discern the Gifts of Leadership and the Planning of Events

Once you have a steering committee in place, the purpose of your initial meeting is to discern what gifts are present in the body you have assembled. Some might have good communication skills or Web skills; others may plan a great party. Some will have professional ministry skills—like the ability to run a retreat or organize a prayer service, Bible study, or day of reflection. Others might suggest things that they'd like to explore and could be willing to do the research in order to plan that event. (One young woman I remember studied the history of our church building for a month and then led a tour of the church for young adults. The event sold out and we continued to do it on a yearly basis.) Once you have an idea of the gifts that are present, you can set a schedule of events to publish everywhere. A good start would be to attempt to do between four and eight events in the course of two "semesters." In my first attempt at young adult ministry with Fathers Hoover and Andrews at St. Paul's, our schedule looked like this:

Sunday, September 19: Kick-off wine and cheese party. After the 5:15 p.m. Mass (Bill and Sharon organize)

Sunday, October 17: Feed the homeless at the Welcome Table at 2 p.m. (Margaret organizes)

Saturday, November 6: Day Retreat in Ossining, NY, 9 a.m. to 6 p.m. (Mike organizes)

Sunday, December 14: Christmas Party (Tara organizes)

Sunday, January 7: Run the Three Kings Epiphany Party for children of the parish (Roberto organizes)

Friday–Sunday, February 4–6: Lenten Retreat, Oak Ridge NJ (Mike and Father Brett organize)

Sunday, March 24: Work in the parish homeless shelter (Bill organizes)

Saturday, April 15: Lecture—The Instant-Replay Mass (Sharon and Father Eric organize). We videotaped a Mass and had Father Eric explain all the parts of the Mass afterwards.

There were four events scheduled for each "semester," and that was plenty for our group of six steering committee members alongside two priests. We averaged about thirty-five people per event, which was not bad for starters, and one young woman named Margaret handled a lot of the direct personal invitations for people. She constantly called people to remind them of events the week before or e-mailed people reminders from time to time. She was always walking up to new people, and her enthusiasm for inviting people was contagious to the rest of the group.

None of this would have been possible without us discerning our gifts early on and finding that some of us had great gifts in organizing retreats, planning community service events, putting together a lecture series, reaching out to people, or simply throwing a great party.

Use Technology in As Many Ways As Possible

This item will be expanded upon in chapter 8, but suffice it to say for now that technology is always changing. When I started in young adult ministry we connected with people mostly by telephone. Suddenly a shift occurred not long after we started, and e-mail became a preferred mode of communication. This occurred over the course of six months to a year. The delivery system is constantly changing with regard to communications technology. Instant messaging gets replaced by text messaging via phone. Blackberry devices become readily available. There are iPods everywhere, and podcasting is becoming just one more mode of communication. In short, you need to be using technology. The following chapter will offer specifics on how to do that.

With Regard to Marketing:
Go Where You Think You Should Not Go;
Do What You Think You Should Not Do

One of the major events in the life of our e-magazine, BustedHalo.com, was booking our first Internet ad on a satirical Web site known as The Onion. Everyone told us we were crazy to advertise on a site that made fun of everyone, including Catholics, and sometimes in a crude way. But we knew that young adults were a constant presence on that site, and the visitors who clicked on that ad became our base audience. We simply went where the target audience was—even when others thought we were crazy to do so.

A campus minister I know booked a local watering hole to do a Theology on Tap session. He picked the place because his college students frequented it. To get the bar for free, he had to pick an off-night, a Tuesday in this instance, to hold his event. So the two weeks before his Tuesday event, what did this young campus minister do? He ran into the bar with posters and beer coasters that had all of the information for his upcoming event. You saw him sitting in the bar with students (all of whom were of drinking age) chatting to them about the event. He even stood outside the bar handing people flyers and other kinds of marketing items (postcards, bookmarks) for the event. People told him he was crazy and that he was promoting drinking. But that bar was packed for his event, and they kept coming after that first event because it was done superbly with excellent hospitality and a wonderful speaker.

Always Be Mindful of the Transcendent

I am always after my own parish in this regard. Our parish is a strong welcoming community, but sometimes we tend to overdo it a bit. We like being around one another, and we find ourselves chatting away in the back of church right up to before the welcome.

During Lent, our choir plays an introit chant before our opening hymn. Often the choir walks in, takes their places, and then just starts the chant. The problem here is that half of the people sitting in the pews have no idea what is going on, and the other half is still engaged in conversation during the chant. It is a good idea that was poorly executed and could be improved by drawing from the Cusick school of "Assume little, explain lots."

However, the thought behind this idea is superb. We do indeed want to call people's attention to the fact that this time is like no other time. We need to literally "call people" into this sense of the transcendent. This means that someone needs to get up, welcome people to church, and then ask for silence — reminding us that we are in sacred space. We need to move this concept into all aspects of our ministry. We need more opportunities to discern where Jesus truly is, and we need to do so in the silence of our hearts, stilling ourselves to listen for that loving voice that lives within us that we call God.

Ask yourself these questions often: Are we praying together enough? Is this ministry or is this merely socializing?

Young adults can socialize anywhere. They hit the bars, they chat on myspace.com and other Internet sites, they frequent clubs and even do service projects together. What they are seeking is something *more*, something beyond the chatter of the bars and the superficial relationships they may be engaged in. With ecumenical relations being what they are today, young adults do not come to a young adult group looking for a marriage partner simply because other young adults are there. Rather, they come because *Catholic* young adults are there. They want to find people who share their Catholic values, people who can pray with them, and people who value Catholic ritual. Catholic young adults flock to places where there are like-minded people who share a love for the Catholic faith.

Second, young adults want opportunities to pray and to be engaged in good ritual moments. Sacramental young adults are not alone in this regard. If they have joined a Catholic young adult group, chances are quite high that they will be interested in opportunities that are specifically Catholic. So opportunities to attend eucharistic adoration, reconciliation services, praise and worship sessions, specialty Masses (like a Mass specifically for young adults), prayer groups, retreats, and Taizé groups are all good offerings for any young adult group and they should be offered frequently.

Always Provide and Emphasize Safe Space

On a blog that I read regularly, certain individuals who'd had a terrible (and justified) experience of retreat ministry were lambasting the sharing that takes place on a retreat. It turns out that they were forced to share their feelings during a retreat, and when they revealed something personal about themselves others gossiped about them when they returned to their university community.

Now while this has never been my personal experience with regard to retreats, I do not doubt that the danger of this happening is certainly more than possible. I wondered why this happened to them and why it never happened to me. I realized quickly that it was because of the value of safe space that had always been emphasized. The young adult leaders present on the retreats modeled this for others, and it became a valued cultural aspect of the retreat community I was and continue to be a part of.

A simple phrase to remember: *What you see here, what you hear here, let it stay here when you leave here.*

The second aspect regards pastoral care. When you are providing pastoral care or counseling, there obviously needs to be some confidentiality established between the client and the counselor. This needs to be communicated to the client, as many do not have an experience of a therapeutic relationship with a religious professional. One priest who does frequent pastoral counseling tells his clients that "my stole is always on when you are in this room."

People need to feel safe and to have that confidentiality honored by leaders. Severe repercussions on college campuses or in parishes occur whenever confidentiality is breached. There are a few instances when an exception can be made here (knowledge of the intent to break the law is one, and endangerment of the life of a patient or another being is another).

What is more is that people need to share their stories with others. We need to be involved with one another for many reasons. We are primarily a more isolated country today. So the opportunity to be with other people is one that connects us not only more closely, but in some cases it may be the only time that we get to talk with people on any kind of a deep level.

Granted, ministers also need to go beyond the experience of sharing for sharing's sake. We share with one another not to be a touchy-feely kind of group, but rather because a fundamental of our faith tradition is to have great concern for one another— to treat each other like brothers and sisters. This too needs to be communicated—especially to the people who are less open to this kind of atmosphere. Ministers need to go beyond sharing activities to provide teaching and new challenges for young adults—but that doesn't mean that we stop sharing altogether. Rather, it means that we need to start with sharing and move to challenging one another privately, but always with concern and compassion for each other.

Always Be Available, Especially during the "Moments of Return"

Time is always of the essence with young adults. Quite often their time is not respected, and because of that they tend not to respect the time restraints of others. Because they expect things at the touch of a button, they also expect that you as a pastoral minister will also be there when they need you. Perhaps this is an unrealistic expectation on their part, but being available when young adults reach out to you is not. A priest friend I know is surprised when people come up to him after Mass and ask him if he has a few minutes to chat sometime. While he is surprised, I am not. Sunday Mass is the only time some of these young people see a priest. Perhaps one of them was moved by that priest's homily that day and spared no time in taking an opportunity to reach out to that priest on a more intimate level. What's more important to note for your own personal health is that in most cases there is no need for an immediate appointment if someone asks for your assistance. A priest friend I know keeps his Palm Pilot on him at all times and even holds it in his hand after Mass, just so he can make appointments with people who ask him for some time. Lay pastoral ministers also need to take advantage of being present at Sunday Mass so that their visible presence at the most vital point in our church's week is a sign of availability to those who seek assistance.

Appreciate Gifts

As we start to get to know people in our parishes, we come to appreciate their gifts and talents. Do we ever invite them to use those talents for the church? I know of a young man with an MBA who has never been asked to sit on the parish's finance council! Another is an actor who has never been approached about becoming a lector. The worst stories come from several young adults who have offered their gifts to the church and were turned away or nobody followed up on the offer (the latter being one of the more frustrating things often reported by young adults).

For those who are able to offer gifts to a given parish, the words "thank you" should be said often. A young adult in one community was running a particular parish program during Holy Week for six consecutive years, and a new pastoral team eliminated it without so much as a thank-you for the past six years. (They also didn't even consult him!) When gifts are appreciated, young adults are most apt to appreciate the gifts you offer with your ministry.

Identify New Leaders

The conventional wisdom says that while doing the work of ministry you should find your replacement. Always be looking for people who are gifted and healthy that have leadership potential and then invite them into that role. It is a constant need in young adult ministry. We pray for vocations all the time. We also need to pray for more young people who can do the work of ministry alongside the clergy. I have a personal rule that I never ask anybody to be a leader that I have seen (or communicated with) only once. If I see someone with a gift for leadership, I notice how they work with others and what gifts and talents they demonstrate over a short period of time. Only then do I extend an invitation.

In young adult ministry groups of which I have been a part, we have also had a roundtable discussion at our follow-up meetings when each person is asked as part of the agenda to name one or two people who they think might be a good replacement for themselves on the steering committee and why. We then discern who we might want to call to leadership for the following year or semester. I have found that others often pointed to gifts that people had that most of us were unaware of. The diversity of the steering committee also helps in this regard, as sacramental young adults might pick similar quiet prayerful types of people, while communal young adults would pick group members who jumped in quickly to pitch in at a service or social event.

In any case, leaders are crucial to the ongoing success of your ministry, so you should choose them with care.

In Your Case, Sunday Is a Workday. In Their Case, It Is Their One Time to Connect with You.

If young adults give you any time at all, that time usually revolves around Sunday Mass. So it is indispensable for you to be present at Sunday Mass, whether lay or clergy. If you are not present at Sunday Mass, most likely neither will the young adults involved in your ministry. Sunday is also a day to let newcomers know about your ministry offerings. If you see a new person at Mass, that is an opportunity to introduce yourself and invite them to an upcoming event after getting to know a bit about them. Ninety percent of the people who are involved in church ministry become engaged in those ministries because they heard about it on a Sunday (probably a conservative estimate). It sounds obvious because it is; we need to use Sunday, the one day that people are actually present in church, to engage them in parish life beyond that one hour of Sunday Mass.

For lay ministers, you should be active in some form of liturgical ministry. That only serves to make you more visible to the parish and besides, it is a good example on your part. We need to invite people into those roles on a more frequent basis, and if you are fulfilling one of those roles it will be that much easier to invite someone else to take part in being a lector or eucharistic minister at Mass.

In my opinion, ministers should "work" Sunday through Thursday and take off Friday and Saturday as a weekend. Sunday, a day of rest for someone else, cannot be a day where ministry grinds to a halt; rather, it is the one crucial day in which ministers need to work harder than ever.

Look at What Other Churches Are Doing

And I don't mean only Catholic ones. Protestant churches are recruiting young adults in droves to their churches. Megachurches are thriving. These churches are experts in marketing and in high-powered ritual services. What can we learn from them? Do we do ritual well? Are we constantly inviting people? What do they require of their members? Why do young adults find this community engaging?

Look at neighboring parishes and see how they do ritual. What do they do poorly? What do they do particularly well? How can your ministry be unique? What can you do that nobody else is doing? What mistakes are they making that we can learn from?

A young adult minister I know noticed that many young adults were engaged by a neighboring Protestant church in his area. He attended a few services to see just what they had to offer. Overall, he found the services to be quite engaging but at times superficial. He implored his pastor to take a good look at the preaching that the parish staff offered and to simply "bring it up a notch." In general, the parish's preaching messages were usually first-rate but the delivery of the material was stale. A small adjustment made a huge difference here and engaged many young adults, who left the popular Protestant church after they found it to be overly superficial.

Second, do not be afraid to team up with another parish to offer something bigger and better than you could do alone. One parish I'm familiar with runs a large welcome banquet for the homeless, and they always invite young adults from other parishes to take part by volunteering. Another parish took it upon themselves to gather all the young adult leaders together from their part of their city to plan a huge conference for all the young adults of the area. Priests in one city I know came together and offered a floating young adult Mass in a different parish each month. We are all on the same team, after all!

The prevailing fear is that young adults will leave your community if they find another community that suits their needs better. That is certainly the case. However, if you have valued young adults, they tend to stay with you, despite the occasional foray into another community for a particular service. My recommendation is to build strong community ties before coupling up with another parish or to intentionally gather neighboring parishes together at the onset of building ministry and deciding what you could all offer together for the young adults in your area (deanery, diocese, etc.).

Provide Challenges

We touched on this when talking about sharing in retreat settings. We must provide a sense of challenge for young people.

They expect to be challenged in their workplace, in educational endeavors, even in building their families.

Do we invite people to take on uncomfortable roles in our parish, like challenging them to visit dying people in the hospital or bringing communion to shut-ins and spending some time with them? One parish invited young adults to visit people in a local hospital's burn unit. Young adults uncomfortably spent time with people who were burned well over 60 percent of their bodies. Needless to say, these people were difficult even to look at, and many of them were in their final days and needed help with coming to terms with their mortality, making sure their families were taken care of, and dealing with the anger that robbed them of their lives. While none of the young adults who served as visitors were psychologists, they were able to simply hold the charred hands of these people in their final hours when nobody else would. They took extra time with the families of these people and took care of many of their needs. Some young adults of great means even helped families financially, bringing much relief to those they visited. Without the challenging suggestion of their young adult minister, this never would have occurred.

A friend mentioned to me recently that we rarely challenge people to move beyond their own ideologies within their comfortable church circles. For example, if young adults are interested in the pro-life movement, how many of those that attend life walks or protests outside abortion clinics are ever asked to take part in lobbying their legislators to change laws that make abortion legal or that put economically poor pregnant women at risk of living in severe poverty? How many are asked to work at a pregnancy crisis center or a home for pregnant teens? The converse is also true: are the people who *would* work to help pregnant teens ever asked to come to a peaceful protest, even if that makes them somewhat uncomfortable?

In our Catholic community there are many things that we might not like doing, but that does not mean that we should not do them at all. We also need to explain why we take part in such events. This leads nicely into my next point.

Highlight the Wisdom of Tradition

Why do we do the things we do? In Linda I.'s interview earlier in this book, she mentioned the fact that she did social justice ministry not simply because it was a nice thing to do but rather because the gospel of Jesus Christ calls her to live in this way. Do we connect that gospel wisdom with the actions of ministry?

In our retreat program, we often have a session called "The Question Box," in which we are able to forthrightly address questions that young adults have without offering them simplistic answers. Rather, we are able to point to our tradition and highlight what that tradition is pointing to as wisdom. We need to point to the fact that the church has thought about these questions for much longer than we have and what's more, they have had some of the most brilliant minds of the modern age considering them and dialoguing with our leaders. With that in mind, we might want to think twice before criticizing the tradition. Because young adults often resort to quick sound bytes as answers, the catechism has served them well in this manner and is enjoying revitalization in our church. However, many young adults are critical of what the catechism says (especially those outside the church doors) and want to know not simply what the catechism says but why. Where did the wisdom come from? This is our opportunity to discuss why the tradition is wise indeed. I often take sexuality as an example in this manner.

Often young people believe that having sex outside of marriage is thought to be sinful in the eyes of the church—but for those who may have experienced sex outside of marriage, their experience tells them that sex is in fact a beautiful thing, and even more so a pleasurable thing. So how do they square their experience with their Catholic faith? The wisdom that the church teaches is not that sex is a dirty or a filthy thing, but rather it is something to be respected, even feared to an extent. Sexuality wields great power—the power to create a new life. This is something not to enter into lightly. When considering sex, we need to ask ourselves if we are ready for the responsibilities that go along with sex. If the answer is no, then we are probably not ready to be that intimate with someone else. To do anything else (use birth control to relieve us of the responsibility, etc.) would be immature and would rob sexuality of its preciousness.

When young adults hear an argument like that, they are more apt to listen to it. They want to know what their tradition speaks, what they are called to be as Catholics, and why that might make sense to them. John Paul II often set the bar high for young adults by explaining much to them about sexuality in particular, and his *Theology of the Body* is often pointed to in many circles as something that young people have great interest in.

Evaluate Your Strengths; Pray for the Future

At this point you will have been able to put together a well-formed young adult ministry program. Your job is not finished. How well did this program work? I would caution that you should evaluate quality and not merely quantity. You may have only gotten six young adults to come to your events, but how did they respond to it? At the same time if you were able to gather four hundred young adults to an event, but a riot broke out at the end of it and they burned down the parish center, that should tell you something too. You will probably fall somewhere between these two extremes.

I use an evaluation method called OLPAF (Our Lady of Protecting All that Follows), which I dedicated to the Blessed Mother. It goes like this:

OBSERVATION: Who came? What happened? Did we do what we set out to do? How well did we do it? How did people respond?

LEADERSHIP: How well did the leaders do? Did they plan everything well? Did they provide good hospitality? Good programming? Did they create safe space if sharing occurred? Did anything go drastically wrong? Did we notice any new leaders at our event?

PRAYERFULNESS: Did we mention Jesus at least once? This sounds obvious, but you would be surprised how often this goes by the wayside! If we did a service event, how did it differ from Habitat for Humanity? If we did a social event, how are we different from the local bar? If there was a speaker, did he or she keep our Catholic principles highlighted, or could the talk have happened at City Hall? In short, how did we *own* this event and how Catholic was it? Have we prayed about where we could go from here and taken steps to do so—not merely wish we could do better? How has our experience empowered us? Did we pray enough together?

AMENDMENTS: What would we do differently? What could we do better? What failed miserably? What didn't go as planned—and was that a good thing? How could we have gotten others involved? What only needs a slight adjustment? What should we do again?

FUTURE: What do we do now? Who do we invite into doing this with us? How do we become more holy because of what we have done, and what have we learned about our faith experience? How will we continue to share this experience with others?

In the end, our evaluations will serve to make our ministry stronger and will also require some humbleness on our part. Not everything we do will be a success, but we need to see that we indeed are not perfect. We are not God but are merely his servants. In serving him, we have learned much about ourselves and about how we can continue to serve him and young adults. Let us pray that we can continue to do good work in his name.

CHAPTER 8

RESOURCES FOR BUILDING A YOUNG ADULT MINISTRY

This chapter outlines resources in building ministry programs for each "type" of young adult. It also provides human resources—groups and other books by people who I have learned from and hold in great esteem. Many of these resources can be found online, and where possible, I have provided the direct links for the resource.

Who's Afraid of the Big Bad Web

The Cowardly Lion in *The Wizard of Oz* reminds me a lot of older campus ministers and religious professionals who are simply too scared to learn about constructing young adult Web resources. It seems that if they "do believe in spooks, they will believe in spooks." To put your mind at ease, you should know that I knew next to nothing about the Web, podcasting, or e-newsletters before I started any of those ventures. I now can edit simple HTML code, construct an XML feed for podcasting, and build a random e-newsletter fairly simply. This is not rocket science. I would recommend taking a simple HTML class if there is one in your area. This is something that I did not do starting out, and it ended up costing me a lot of money in the long term. The basics are pretty easy. I often recommend several of the books in the Dummies series, and there is a *Web Design for Dummies* book (which you can get through Amazon.com—just type "Web Design for Dummies" in the search box and hit GO) that could be well worth the cost of picking up and familiarizing yourself with. Also check out the book *HTML for Dummies*.

The Internet Is for...

Before I explore each type of young adult, I would like to mention a bit about ministry on the Internet, which I have avoided up until this point in the book. While I believe that Internet ministry is crucial in ministry with young adults, it also never replaces the human touch. Like most things on the Internet, these resources enhance your ministry but never really replace it, unless you decide to run an Internet magazine like BustedHalo.com (www.bustedhalo.com) or a blog like Amy Welborn's Open Book (http://amywelborn.typepad.com/openbook/). The Internet serves us mostly as an informational source or opportunity to dialogue where distance and time would not allow an immediate connection to take place. That being said, I will offer tips on building a simple parish Web site, a blog, a podcast, an electronic newsletter, and even an Internet magazine, and offer some suggestions to accentuate these Web resources with additional pastoral solutions.

Parish Young Adult Web Site

There is an easy and a hard way to construct a Web site for your young adult ministry. The easy way is to have someone construct a simple one for you, while the hard way is to construct it yourself or pay a whole lot of money to someone else to build one with a lot of bells and whistles.

A main question to ask yourself: What do you want to want to do with the Web site? What purpose does it serve? Building a Web site for your group may actually not be necessary. Some cheaper solutions could suffice. But let us pick some obvious reasons why you would want a young adult Web site.

a. *To post event listings:* This is the main reason why people construct young adult Web sites. They build an online calendar for their events, Mass times, etcetera.

b. *To connect young adults with resources:* There are many online resources out there for young adults, and many people simply list those Web resources on a links page or some other way.

c. *To answer questions:* Some young adult Web sites feature questions that young adults e-mail in to a priest or a young adult minister, and they post the answers online. BustedHalo.com has a version of this called "Ask Father Joe," which you can find here: http://www.bustedhalo. com/ask_father_joe/index.htm

d. *To have an online chat or discussion:* Chat rooms and discussion boards are two ways of interacting online. Chat rooms are basically real-time discussions online. People simply type or in some cases speak (which is called a voice chat) to others on a Web site live. At times the discussions are moderated and others are more free-flowing, depending on the wishes of the moderators (or chat host).

Discussion boards differ in that they are not held in real time. They are basically online bulletin boards where people can post their comments or respond to previous ones.

Obviously our first reason will be the most prevalent. We want people to receive information on our ministry. If this is the only reason you want a Web site, then there are several easy solutions:

1. *Get a page on your parish (or diocesan or religious order) Web site:* If your parish already has a Web site, then simply ask the webmaster if he can assign a page for young adult ministry. He can then show you how to update your page by using a simple administrative feature, or he can simply ask you to send him the information and update it on his (or her) own. I would caution the use of the latter option. Webmasters are busy people, and they might not be able to update your page as swiftly as you might like them to. But getting the page itself on an existing Web site is possibly a free solution for you.

2. *Catholicweb.com:* This is one of the many free solutions that exist for parishes that want a simple Web site. Catholicweb.com will produce a simple Web site for you free of charge in exchange for your carrying their advertisers on your Web page. (Author's note: All of the advertisers are approved by Catholicweb, so they do not pander to sites that your parish may find distasteful.) The pages are simple and they will tell you how you can best manage your site. There are not many bells and whistles to these sites, so they are simple and easy to navigate — which is always preferable to "nice looking, but I can't find anything on it."

3. *Find a young adult to design your site:* In the midst of your young adult group there is bound to be a person who knows how to build a simple Web page. Some will even do it free for you, so they'll be sharing their gifts and talents with their parish community. Be careful though; once they build it, you may have to update it. They may not have the time to teach you how.

4. *Pay a design firm to design your site and pick a URL name:* This is the most expensive solution, however, if it is important to you to have a great looking Web site

with all of the features I listed above, then you might want to go this route. You will also need someone to "host" your site. That is, the site needs to "live on the Internet somewhere." Your design company might indeed also offer hosting services, but most likely you will have to go to another company and pay them a monthly fee for hosting.

Once you have a design firm and a host, you will need a name for your Web site. I would suggest not being too creative here. You want people to remember your site's name, but also you want it to be clearly associated with your ministry. So if you belong to St. Paul's Young Adult Ministry, a good "URL name" (the name people refer to as a Web site name) might be www.stpaulsyoungadult-ministry.org. If that name is already taken, you might want to add your city or state to the URL (for example, www.stpaulsyoungadultministrynewyorkcity.org). If your ministry has a specific name, then that should be your URL (such as, www.westsiders.com, or www.yaggies.org).

Simpler Solutions: Blogs and E-Newsletters

What is a blog? Blog is short for Web log, which is basically an online diary. Most blogs are simply meanderings from a specific person and are usually written from a particular point of view. If you basically want a place on the Web where you are able to post your ministry's latest events and maybe provide some entertaining comments or news items of interest, then a blog may indeed be a good solution.

The good news is that blogs are free and so simple to set up that a child could do it. Check out Blogger (http://www.blogger. com), Typepad (www.typepad.com), or Wordpad (www.wordpad.

com) for some simple blogging software. (*Author's note:* While all three sites "walk you" through the process, I find Blogger the easiest to use.)

Why Blog?

Blogging takes advantage of an old media genre. Rush Limbaugh capitalized on the idea of "interpreting the news for his audience." Blogs do something similar in many cases. I find there are three types of blogs in general:

a. *News Blogs.* These are blogs that update their audiences on news items thought to be of interest, and the authors of these blogs usually offer their opinionated comments on them (in other words, they interpret the news for you). In the case of the church, bloggers often use their blogs as a way to transmit the latest information about what is going on in the church and offer their comments on that news.

b. *Diablogs.* These are blogs in which there is more than one person posting as the main author. Often two people are discussing a number of daily news topics with their own particular spin on them.

c. *Mindless rants.* I say that with all due respect—some bloggers simply vent their thoughts in a stream of consciousness manner. It is an undisciplined form of writing that merely expresses the first instinct of the author without any reflection.

I read some blogs regularly and find them to be excellent sources of information, even if I don't always agree with the authors' stances. They are:

Open Book by Amy Welborn:
http://amywelborn.typepad.com/openbook/

This is one of the better church news blogs out there. Amy always has the latest news and is a frequent contributor to the *New York Times* and other area papers. She has also authored many books. The blog itself is always just right of center but never extreme.

Whispers in the Loggia by Rocco Palmo:
http://whispersintheloggia.blogspot.com

This is a creative blog that offers rumors and hard news straight out of the Vatican. Palmo is also a regular contributor to BustedHalo.com with a biweekly column called "Almost Holy." Rocco, a young Millennial adult, knows everything there is to know about the Vatican and is entertaining as he tells us about it. He gives equal time to dishing the dirt that everyone wants the inside scoop on.

You Duped Me, Lord by Mark Mossa, SJ:
http://markmossasj.blogspot.com/

The further adventures of a thirty-something Jesuit. Mark is a Jesuit seminarian who is often funny and insightful. He sometimes takes snippets of St. Ignatius's Spiritual Exercises and offers some excellent reflections on these passages.

Busted Blog:
http://www.bustedhalo.com/bustedblog/?cat+77

This is BustedHalo.com's blog, which contains several authors who blog from many points of view. I started it and moderate the discussion.

Dot Commonweal by the editors of *Commonweal* Magazine
http://www.commonwealmagazine.org/blog/

This is the blog of *Commonweal* magazine. The topics are often very interesting, and all sides of the Catholic spectrum weigh in with insightful comments on the matters discussed. A liberal bias is often clear from the standpoint of the contributors, but do not be fooled. The comments behind the main page are often charged with great arguments, and good points are made from both sides of the debates.

Heart, Mind and Strength by Greg Popcak (and others):
http://www.exceptionalmarriages.com/weblog/

This is a news blog with a host of contributors. Much of the news is timely and often insightful, encompassing events that are happening around the country. Like Dot Commonweal, this is a fairly stilted blog from the opposite perspective. However, much of the information is timely, funny, and oftentimes with a unique spin on given situations. Even when I do not agree with the ideology presented, I find it insightful to read.

Naturally I have my own blog called Googling God (googlinggod.blogspot.com), which is much like some of the above. It contains comments on items that I find interesting within the church, where I am speaking, conferences that I think would be rewarding, and just general meanderings.

If you want to create a blog simply to keep in touch with your young adult ministry crew and inform them of events, my suggestion is to blog regularly…daily or at least three to four times a week. A short reflection on the daily readings is not a bad idea for a blog item. My old blog, Proverbial Wisdom, used to contain a single reflection on a single proverb once per day. Blogs are short and quick news items. If you are blogging pages of material, then you do not get the idea. Information that is disseminated quickly is the key here. So this can indeed be a quick way to keep young adults up to date on information that you find valuable and events for them to attend.

Electronic Newsletters and E-Mail Blasts

The beauty of the e-newsletter is that people receive them right in the inboxes of their e-mail. The hard part of the e-newsletter is that you need people to subscribe to it. An e-newsletter is simply an HTML-designed e-mail that is sent to the inboxes of people who subscribe to the newsletter. The concept of the e-newsletter is simple. When you have a Web site or a blog, you depend on people to continue to visit your site. The only solution to drive people to your site is word of mouth, a link from another site, or advertising. But what if people decided to share their e-mail address with you and allowed you to send them an update when you had crucial information that you wanted them to see. In the case of my ministry's Internet magazine, BustedHalo.com, we send out a weekly e-newsletter detailing our most current stories. Now you are no longer depending on people to go to your Web site, rather you are sending the information to them directly. Two types of e-newsletter programs that I recommend are called Vertical Response (http://www.verticalresponse.com) and Constant Contact (http://www.constantcontact.com). Both programs are user friendly and provide the wherewithal to construct a simple e-newsletter with little effort. You only pay for the number of e-mails that you send out. In some cases if you have a small list of people that you want to remain in contact with, the cost may be free (constant contact is free for fifty or fewer people at last check). Otherwise the cost is roughly 0.5 cent per e-mail — however, the more e-mail you send, the cheaper the cost per e-mail. BustedHalo.com uses Constant Contact and sends over fifty thousand e-mails to subscribers per year at an inexpensive cost of $500. If you snail mailed a newsletter you would probably pay a lot more than that for postage. This is a simple and ingenious way to continue to distribute information quickly and cheaply with little effort. All you need to do is gather the e-mail addresses of those who are active in your ministry group and get their permission to send them your newsletter. Permission is important. There are a lot of SPAM laws now that you don't want to violate.

An e-mail blast can be a bit different. Certain e-mail programs will allow you to send bulk e-mail to a certain number of e-mail addresses (in most cases not more than a hundred or so). You can just construct a simple e-mail message with the information you would like to share and add the e-mail addresses to a listing of recipients. Some people also set up what is known as a listserv, which is an e-mail address that you can write to and it will distribute your comments to others that have subscribed to the same list. Others set up a group listing through Yahoo Groups (http://groups.yahoo.com/). In short, there is no reason for you not to be using one or more of these programs for communication. It could not be simpler, and young adults use these programs constantly. Not to use them is to simply be rendered irrelevant.

Podcasting

This is the latest venture that Father Dave Dwyer and I at BustedHalo.com have started. Podcasting takes its name from the iPod, Apple Computer's mp3 player that has become very popular. Somewhere along the line the idea of producing simple talk shows of about five to thirty minutes in length that people could listen to on their iPods got very popular. In short, you simply record an audio file, create what is known as an enclosure feed, and then host that file on an Internet site somewhere, and voila! You have created your very own talk show. Listeners subscribe using an audio aggregator like iTunes or iPodder, and the latest show automatically downloads into their computers. So each time they connect their iPods to their computers they get the latest show on their devices. Father Dave and I host the BustedHalo Cast twice a week, and we get a real kick out of it. We are both former radio guys, so we brought some expertise to this already. Still, most of the podcasts I hear are not very professionally produced. It seems that the standards for podcasting are not all that high in terms of broadcast quality, but you *should* aim high. Father Roderick, who hosts both Daily Breakfast and Catholic Insider, two of the more popular podcasts, travels all around the world recording everything from interviews at World Youth Day to just his own enthusiastic meanderings.

Why podcast? Simply put, young people are looking for connections and direction in their lives, and with their busy schedule a thirty-minute podcast might be a simple way for them to check in with God for the day. Many of our listeners in New York and Boston listen on their subway run to work. Others listen while running or working out at the gym. It is a way to get into the busy schedule of young adults fairly easily.

Content

What can you podcast? Virtually anything. Our weekly podcast, the BustedHalo Cast, consists of Father Dave Dwyer and me answering a weekly question. Another colleague, Father Rick Walsh, provides us with a spiritual almanac chock full of spiritual information for a particular date. One of our editorial assistants does street interviews on a spiritual topic, and we recommend a church from somewhere in the nation on our acclaimed church search. We also have guest interviews from time to time (Jimmy Carter and Anne Rice are two of the more famous names who have come by). We are always thinking of new things as well.

However, you need not get this creative. Priests can podcast their latest homilies. Creative lectors can simply read the Sunday readings in a dramatic fashion. One podcast simply has the rosary or the liturgy of the hours being recited! Simple solutions are sometimes best. The British Jesuits have an excellent podcast called Pray As You Go (http://www.pray-as-you-go.org), which focuses on a simple method of Ignatian prayer in audio form that you can download to your iPod. They include great contemplative sounds and songs as well.

Constructing Podcasts

Some good resources to help with building your podcast:

1. *Podcast Solutions:* This book (http://www.amazon.com —type "Podcast Solutions" in the search box, and hit GO) is the bible of podcasting. Dan Klass and Michael Geoghegan have written an easy-to-use, step-by-step guide to podcasting that's so simple even a child could do it. Father Dave and I used this book, and it gave us all the material we needed from equipment ideas to how to create an XML feed. It was an indispensable guide for us.

2. Liberated Syndication or Libsyn: Liberated Syndication is a premiere media distribution service that provides cheap hosting space and a simple blog for your podcast. This will save you a lot of money and time in the long run. You now do not need a Web site to host your podcast. Podcasts take up a lot of bandwidth space, which is expensive for you since your hosting company charges you for it. Libsyn.com allows you to put your podcasts on their server for a reduced price.

3. Freeplay Music: Check out this music source on the Web that has "safe to play" music for podcasts. There are rights issues with certain songs, so you cannot play the

latest hits on your podcast without permission of the major labels. Freeplay allows you to use their music, which has been cleared to play without any rights fees.

Internet Magazines

I doubt many of you would rush out to create a full-scale Internet magazine like BustedHalo.com, but we did indeed start our national ministry to young adults with this venture. Our magazine is part static faith information and part magazine articles for spiritual seekers. We publish one new story per day of about seven or eight hundred words and have writers from all over the country contributing. In our case, the site we built is so huge that we hired a firm to help us design it, and we spared no expense in trying to make it look very professional. Most of you will not need a site this big. However, should you want to attempt something like this, I would recommend spending the money and using a Web design firm.

Internet magazines also need to have short engaging articles and be easily navigable. You should design your site as simply as possible with useful navigation bars and all of the main material you hope to share front and center on your homepage. You should also include a section called "About Us," where people can find out who you are and what your ministry is about.

One of the reasons that BustedHalo grew in popularity is that we simply do not preach to the choir. We try to talk about issues that people who might not darken the door of a church are interested in, and then we try to connect those issues with spirituality. How does God fit in with my work or relationships? Where does spirituality fit in with politics or pop culture?

We also do not dodge issues. We talked about the sex abuse crisis, gays in the priesthood, Opus Dei, the silencing of a Catholic magazine editor, and even have a regular sex columnist ("Pure Sex, Pure Love") talk about the struggles of young adult sexuality. That has gained us respect among many young adults who do not expect to regularly find open dialogue about these issues on a Catholic Web site.

In short, Catholic Internet magazines should be edgy, perhaps even generate discomfort at times. They need to engage real issues and at the very least make people think deeply about the issues. They can also provide solid answers to Catholic teaching in other ways, such as we do with our "Faith Guides" section, where we provide snippets of information on the Mass, the Bible, prayer, and even give you a little Catholic trivia game to play. We also have a section where you can ask questions of our spiritual guru, Father Joe. I think that is a piece almost everyone can do. You will never run short on questions (I get about twelve a week).

Other Internet magazines/Web sites I find interesting and useful include:

The Revealer (http://www.therevealer.org/)—A daily review of religion and the press.

Godspy.com (http://www.godspy.com)—Much like Busted-Halo, this magazine compiles articles from other sources and adds some original material to it as well.

American Catholic (http://www.americancatholic.org/)—The site of the St. Anthony Messenger Press, this magazine has great information on it, such as "Saint of the Day," online retreats, and minute meditations.

Beliefnet.com (http://beliefnet.com)—This is not a Catholic site, but rather a site that explores a lot of different spiritual journeys. There is a strong Catholic section, however, that always contains excellent materials and articles. Take their "Belief-o-matic Quiz"!

Sacred Space (http://www.sacredspace.ie)—This is the Web site of the Irish Jesuits, who provide a daily meditation based on the Ignatian Examen. If you want a quick way to get young adults engaged in a daily prayer experience, here is one that they can do right at their computer terminals. Peaceful and serene, each meditation is a great daily opportunity to reconnect with the divine.

Rejesus (http://www.rejesus.com)—A British site that simply explores Jesus. Profound audio and video meditations including a superb one on the seven last sayings of Christ.

Ship of Fools (http://ship-of-fools.com)—A hysterical site from the Anglicans that pokes fun at many aspects of religion. Snarky, but not condescending. There is an underlying respect for the faith journey here amidst the giggles.

NCYAMA (www.ncyama.org)—The site of the National Catholic Young Adult Ministry organization. This is a newly overhauled site with loads of resources on it along with the latest job listings for young adult ministry professionals. If you are a young adult minister you should absolutely become a member of this organization. They put on a can't-miss forum for young adult leaders every year that is always solid.

Books

If you are looking for good resources to read about the young adult experience, there are several books I would recommend as must-reads:

1. *The Basic Guide to Young Adult Ministry* by Father John Cusick and Katherine DeVries
   Everything you ever wanted to know about running a young adult ministry. Cusick is the founder of Theology on Tap and has been a leader in the field for over twenty-five years.

2. *Young Adult Catholics: Religion in the Culture of Choice* by Dean Hoge, William Dinges, Mary Johnson, and Juan Gonzalez

   A groundbreaking sociological study from the year 2000. Much of their findings are still valid and reveal a good amount about Gen X Catholics. Hoge should be releasing a new study relatively soon.

3. *The New Faithful: Why Young Adults Are Returning to Christian Orthodoxy* by Colleen Carroll

   An anecdotal study on the return of certain young adults to a more orthodox worldview that, while disproved on a larger sociological scale, does accurately portray the sacramental and evangelical sects of young adults within the Catholic Church.

4. *God on the Quad* by Naomi Schaefer Riley

   An examination of today's religious colleges and universities in which Schaefer Riley visits and reports on several — from Yeshiva to Thomas More College — and leaves no stone unturned in her investigation. Her findings are both frightening and inspiring; it is the most accurate description of life on many of the extreme religious schools' campuses. One small quibble: not enough on some of the less extreme religious schools.

5. *Virtual Faith* and *Consuming Faith* (two books) by Thomas Beaudoin

   A good meandering through the world of pop culture and young adulthood. Beaudoin shows how young adults are saturated in the world of popular culture, and in *Consuming Faith* (which I found to be the better of the two books) he talks about the branding culture that they live in.

6. *Losing Your Religion, Finding Your Faith* by Father Brett Hoover, CSP

A groundbreaking work that all spiritual seekers should read. Hoover suggests that young adults need to break away from the religion of their parents to form their own personal faith. Father Brett and I worked together for five years.

7. *Personal Vocation: God Calls Everyone by Name* by Germain Grisez and Russell Shaw
One of the better books I have read on vocational discernment. Very traditional without being extreme, and holds both Gen X and Millennial values in healthy tension. Draws from a variety of resources (from Dorothy Day, the founder of the Catholic Worker movement, to St. Josemaria Escriva, the founder of Opus Dei).

8. *Getting a Life: How to Find Your True Vocation* by Renée LaReau
Another excellent vocational discernment book for young adults. LaReau's offering here is filled with strong stories of decision making from real life. Often heartwarming while remaining challenging, LaReau has a gift of placing her readers at the center of these stories to help them discern where indeed they may wish to turn in their vocational endeavors.

9. *Big Questions, Worthy Dreams* by Sharon Daloz Parks
I often think this book should be entitled *What I Learned from My Students*. Dr. Parks's book centers on the value of mentoring young adults, especially those who are entering and leaving college.

10. *Virtues for Ordinary Christians* by Father James Keenan, SJ
A short book on morality that centers on the theological virtues. Keenan weaves a thoughtful and useful guide for those of us who encounter moral conundrums in our lives and offers some very insightful cues for solving them.

A Final Thought: Your Best Resource Is You

Young adults need your time, your open heart, and your patience. Ministry with this group can often be a thankless job in which you give much more than you receive. But know that you are doing not merely a valuable service to young adults but to the church. Young adults are the biggest demographic that we would consider both unchurched and inactive in our times. It is a vital ministry. In a world that often tells young adults that they don't matter, that they are just another cog in the wheel, or that they are worthless, you can be the lone voice crying in the wilderness that speaks volumes to them.

My very first retreat experience with young adults provided me with a leadership opportunity nearly immediately. I was confronted with a woman who had been brutally abused in her life and who had been embarrassed by a fellow retreat member in the opening minutes of the retreat. I rode up in the car with her on the way and merely made some small talk with her. She had asked to see me for some private counseling just minutes after her embarrassing moment, and a flood of tears came barreling out of her! When our brief session ended, I asked her why she came to me when there were certainly many other qualified people on the staff who could probably offer her much more than I could as a neophyte. She remarked, "I trusted you because you made me so comfortable on the ride up here. I just knew you were the right person for me to speak with."

Those are the moments we need to share. Like Jesus, who washed the filthy and disgusting feet of his closest friends as a servant, we must come before those we serve. We need to be willing to touch the rawest and most vulnerable parts of the young adults we come in contact with because the world tells them that they are in need of constant protection.

Our world is also one of vast polarization. Perhaps with this small insight into the differences between generations we can begin to see that we are not as divided as we think we are. We merely have highlighted the cultures of two different generational groups in our past approaches to ministry. We need to try to bring wholeness to our ministry endeavors and in turn let them be a model for the rest of the church. We indeed can be the "common ground" that Cardinal Bernardin hoped for in the not so distant past. All we have to do is simply embrace the Google culture with a human heart.

Young Adults are out there googling God. I pray that you will be someone they find when they do.

AFTERWORD

An article written not too long ago by Fr. John Cusick was entitled "Young Adults—A New Age in the Church." When it was published, there was an expressed concern that the author was endorsing the "new age" movement in our society and lobbying for the church to adapt to a "new age" theology. Nothing was farther from the truth.

The point was that young adult Catholics in their twenties and thirties, both married and single, are a new age of people in the church. These two decades of younger people are more unlike people of that same age range than ever before.

In today's world, and hence in today's church, young adults receive more information about life "online" than anyone else. Theirs is a world of Web sites, e-mails, blogs, search engines (like Google), and instant worldwide communication. They are making print media, newspaper, magazines, and books appear to be from the dinosaur age.

"My space" is no longer defined as a designated parking place at a work site or in a family garage. "Myspace" is now a universally hallowed Web site used by millions of twentysomethings to communicate, blog, write, respond, learn, argue, debate, challenge, and even pray with peers.

However, in a young adult world where so much time is spent in front of a screen, the more things have changed, many more things not only have remained the same but have increased in value and desire.

So many young adults speak of a spiritual hunger. They present to us who minister to them a curiosity and a need to learn about their own religious traditions. The loneliness of sitting in front of a computer screen has prompted a hunger for community, a desire to meet and get connected with people of similar values, faith, and longings.

Googling God: The Religious Landscape of People in their 20s and 30s has presented us with a dual dimensional skill to reach out to Catholic young adults: the method for a ministerial outreach to young adults through local faith communities and the understanding of this new, sometimes strange, technological world. New skills are needed to present our Catholic faith, our religious and spiritual practices, to this world of young adults via the screens directly in front of them. Mike Hayes has enabled us to understand this technological world and the tragic events of the past few years more deeply and critically.

Hayes has also offered us the wisdom and skills he has developed through his remarkable work in reaching out to young adults via BustedHalo.com. And, using contemporary technology, he has presented us with time-tested ways to develop effective ministerial outreaches to this new age in the church.

I hope you will use this book in your work and ministry to young adults. If so, you will allow the work of Mike Hayes to transform "myspace" from a Web site to a faith community gathered together in Jesus' name.

> *Reverend John Cusick*
> Director, Young Adult Ministry
> Archdiocese of Chicago
> Coauthor, *The Basic Guide to Young Adult Ministry*

NOTES

Chapter 1

1. Jackson W. Carroll and Wade Clark Roof, *Bridging Divided Worlds: Generational Cultures in Congregations* (San Francisco: Jossey-Bass, 2002), 63.

2. Ibid.

3. Ibid., 65.

4. Ibid., 67.

5. See Harvey Cox, *Seduction of the Spirit* (New York: Simon and Schuster, 1973), 100–101.

6. Colleen Carroll, *The New Faithful: Why Young Adults Are Returning to Christian Orthodoxy* (Chicago: Loyola Press, 2002), 14.

7. William Dinges et al., *Young Adult Catholics: Religion in the Culture of Choice* (Notre Dame, IN: University of Notre Dame, 2001), 60–61.

8. James Bacik, *Reflections* 26, no. 9 (Toledo, OH: May 2004): 2.

Chapter 2

1. Andrew Greeley, personal interview, via e-mail, March 14, 2005.

2. John Cusick and Kate DeVries, *The Basic Guide to Young Adult Ministry* (Maryknoll, NY: Orbis Books, 2001), 65.

3. Tom Beaudoin, *Virtual Faith: The Irreverent Spiritual Quest of Generation* X (San Francisco: Jossey-Bass, 1998), 17.

Chapter 3

1. Dean Hoge, Theology on Tap Conference, Chicago, October 13, 2005.

Chapter 4

1. Michael Buckley, "Within the Holy Mystery" in *World of Grace*, ed. Leo J. O'Donovan (Washington, DC: Georgetown University Press, 1995), 39–40.
2. http://religion-cults.com/spirit/charismatic.htm

Chapter 6

1. Karl Rahner, *Foundations of Christian Faith* (New York: Crossroad, 1978), 32.
2. Michael Buckley, "Within the Holy Mystery," in *World of Grace*, ed. Leo J. O'Donovan (Washington, DC: Georgetown University Press, 1995), 38–39.
3. Ibid., 39–40.
4. Anne E. Carr, "Starting with the Human," in *World of Grace*, ed. Leo J. O'Donovan (Washington, DC: Georgetown University Press, 1995), 19.
5. Dean Hoge, "Center of Catholic Identity," *National Catholic Reporter*, September 30, 2005, at www.ncronline.org/NCR_online/archives2/2005c/093005/093005k.htm.

6. Peter J. Schneller, "Discovering Jesus Christ: A History We Share," in *World of Grace,* ed. Leo J. O'Donovan (Washington, DC: Georgetown University Press, 1995), 102.

7. Karl Rahner, *Theological Investigations,* vol. 7 (London: Darton, Longman, and Todd, 1971), 9.

8. Ibid., 109.

9. Ibid., 251.

10. James Bacik, *Reflections* 26, no. 9 (Toledo, OH: May 2004): 2.

11. Karl Rahner, *The Shape of the Church to Come* (New York: Crossroad, 1983), 42.

12. Ibid., 61.

13. Ibid., 100–101.

BIBLIOGRAPHY

Bacik, James. *Reflections* 26, no 9. Toledo, OH. (May 2004).

Beaudoin, Tom. *Virtual Faith: The Irreverent Spiritual Quest of Generation X*. San Francisco: Jossey-Bass, 1998.

Buckley, Michael. "Within the Holy Mystery." In *World of Grace*, ed. Leo O'Donovan. Washington, DC: Georgetown University Press, 1995.

Carr, Anne E. "Starting with the Human." In *World of Grace*, ed. Leo O'Donovan. Washington, DC: Georgetown University Press, 1995.

Carroll, Colleen. *The New Faithful: Why Young Adults Are Returning to Christian Orthodoxy*. Chicago: Loyola Press, 2002.

Carroll, Jackson W., and Wade Clark Roof. *Bridging Divided Worlds: Generational Cultures in Congregations*. San Francisco: Jossey-Bass, 2002.

Cusick, John, and Kate DeVries. *The Basic Guide to Young Adult Ministry*. Maryknoll, NY: Orbis Books, 2001.

Greeley, Andrew. Personal interview, March 14, 2005.

Hoge, Dean R., William Dinges, Juan Gonzalez, and Mary Johnson. *Young Adult Catholics: Religion in the Culture of Choice*. South Bend, IN: University of Notre Dame, 2001.

Hoge, Dean. "Center of Catholic Identity." *National Catholic Reporter*, September 30, 2005.

———. Theology on Tap Conference. Chicago: October 13, 2005.

Rahner, Karl. *Foundations of Christian Faith*. New York: Crossroad, 1978.

———. *The Shape of the Church to Come*. New York: Crossroad, 1983.

_____. *Theological Investigations.* Vol. 7. London: Darton, Longman, and Todd, 1971.

Religion-cults.com (Religion-cults.com/spirit/charismatic.htm).

Schneller, Peter J. "Discovering Jesus Christ: A History We Share." In *World of Grace*, ed. Leo O'Donovan. Washington, DC: Georgetown University Press, 1995.